T0283290

THE AUTOBIOGRAPHY OF JOSHUA CHAMBERLAIN

JOSHUA CHAMBERLAIN
EDITED BY THOMAS A. DESJARDIN

Camden, Maine

Down East Books

An imprint of The Globe Pequot Publishing Group, Inc.
64 South Main Street
Essex, CT 06426
www.globepequot.com

Distributed by NATIONAL BOOK NETWORK

British Library Cataloguing in Publication Information available

Library of Congress Cataloging-in-Publication Data
Names: Chamberlain, Joshua Lawrence, 1828-1914. | Desjardin, Thomas A.,
    1964- editor. | Chamberlain, Joshua Lawrence, 1828-1914. My Story of
    Fredericksburg. | Chamberlain, Joshua Lawrence, 1828-1914. Through Blood
    & Fire at Gettysburg. | Chamberlain, Joshua Lawrence, 1828-1914.
    Appomattox.
Title: The autobiography of Joshua Chamberlain / Thomas A. Desjardin.
Description: Camden, Maine : Down East Books, [2025] | Includes
    bibliographical references.
Identifiers: LCCN 2024021134 (print) | LCCN 2024021135 (ebook) | ISBN
    9781684752263 (cloth) | ISBN 9781684752270 (ebook)
Subjects: LCSH: Chamberlain, Joshua Lawrence, 1828-1914. | Generals—United
    States—Biography. | United States. Army—Biography. | Brewer
    (Me.)—Biography. | United States—History—Civil War,
    1861-1865—Personal narratives. | United States. Army. Maine Infantry
    Regiment, 20th (1862-1865)
Classification: LCC E467.1.C47 A3 2025 (print) | LCC E467.1.C47 (ebook) |
    DDC 973.7/441092 [B]—dc23/eng/20240617
LC record available at https://lccn.loc.gov/2024021134
LC ebook record available at https://lccn.loc.gov/2024021135

CONTENTS

1

THE AUTOBIOGRAPHY

~

More than eighty-five years passed between his birth and the end of the remarkable life of Joshua Lawrence Chamberlain. In the early 1890s, when the most dramatic of his life events were behind him, and for reasons he never made clear, he began drafting the story of that life. This autobiography, written when he was nearly sixty years old, is a revealing and candid description of that life from its beginnings in rural Maine through his arrival in a military camp outside Portland in 1862. The manuscript likely ends there because, by 1890, he had already published many articles about his life after that period so that retelling them in an autobiography would merely be duplication.

Various copies of the seventy-seven typescript pages are now in the George Mitchell Archives at Bowdoin College and the National Civil War Museum in Harrisburg, Pennsylvania. Bowdoin College published an edited version of this work in its Orient *magazine in 1992 and in book form as* Blessed Boyhood *in 2013.*

The entire work is presented here, complete with typographical and grammatical errors and words that Chamberlain struck through. Explanatory footnotes have been added throughout.

BACKGROUND

In early fall of 1828, Joshua Lawrence Chamberlain, Jr., and his wife, Sarah, his bride of less than a year, welcomed their first child, a boy whom they named Lawrence. The father, a young lumberman in a region of Maine on the verge of an enormous lumber boom, named him after naval Captain James Lawrence who took command of an American frigate at Boston harbor, sailed it to sea, and immediately

engaged a blockading naval frigate. Lawrence, who was mortally wounded during the
engagement, is said to have told his men, "Don't give up the ship!" as they carried
him below decks. The heroic captain's young namesake became the second generation
of Chamberlains to be born in Brewer, Maine, on the opposite riverbank from the
small but growing city of Bangor. The river between them was made unnavigable
upstream by a set of falls that prevented further sailing into the vast Maine woods.
Within three decades, this river community would export more lumber than any
other port in the world.

Though it was isolated geographically, the merchants and seamen of the area
traveled to port from South America to Europe and beyond, returning, when fair
seas and piracy allowed, with products and sea tales that far exceeded those otherwise
found in the Maine woods. A sailing ship could reach Portland in a day or Boston
in two, when weather permitted, while passengers and mail traveled daily to the coast
by stage. Here, the story of his life in his own words and style of writing begins.

$$\sim$$

THE EARLIEST YEARS

On the bank of the Penobscot, thirty miles above the Bay, at the foot of
the falls—which in the Maine rivers mark so suddenly the head of naviga-
tion—opposite the eastern side of the beautiful and busy city of Bangor,
some freak of nature left a monumental headland. Fronting the river with
a foothold of some six hundred yards at the water's edge, the bold outline
covers many curious beds, on the western flank a vast bank of clay; in the
middle portion mingled with deep drifts of sand and gravel holding in their
embrace far-fetched boulders various in size, shape and composition, all
so loosely held that once broken the spring floods wash away the surface
in great slides to shallow the shelving shores; while the eastern shoulder
rises sharp and sheer—a ledge of solid bluestone the thin mould upon it
scarcely supporting the stunted cedars and pines and hemlocks which cling
to its rugged face, and cast their somber shadows upon the great, dark
river rolling swift and silent three-hundred feet below. Rearward, from
the south, the far swelling slopes stretch upward so gradually that one
approaching from that quarter would hardly be aware of the ascent until
he found himself upon the summit, at the very brink of the bank, where
foot and eye alike are constrained to pause. Before him, across the waters,
he would look down upon the picturesque cluster of buildings which fifty
years ago foretold the coming city, already pushing out and upward from

its life-center, the Kenduskeag,* like a golden lily from its calyx.† From this height, beyond the near horizon, misty mountain peaks stand out under the shining skies like clue-caped outposts watching the unseen distances. Beneath him, the river, for six miles up and down full-seen or caught in gleams and flashes;—on the one hand rafts of great mast-pines and sawed lumber rushing well-guided through the rips to the busy harbor and docks below; on the other, the long procession of white-winged brigs and schooners bringing in domestic and "West India" goods; and perchance a taller bark with rich violence from East Indian or Pacific seas and bearing away the simple products of the forests and fields. The lower shores well lined with shipyards, smelling sweet with fresh hewed timber and new-laid tar, and thrilling the senses with the drumbeat of axe and saw, and adze and sledge. From this height what visions are vouchsafed! What sweep of thoughts.

Here is the launching-scene, joy-day of the children—crowds of well-wishing neighbors—the thoughtful owners—the care-faced master builder, anxious for all things, prompt to knock away the last wedges on the crisis of the tide! The bold builders, to secure the favor of the ground, setting the hull so high that to meet even the fifteen-foot tide it goes down to its embrace with a leap and a bound. Boon of boyhood, to be permitted to "be launched on board"; for so one proves he can stand up for himself, come what shock will. And then the taut stays, the graceful spars, the bright rigging rove aloft, lifting the soul of youth to dream of unheard-of things! Nor wait for the interpreter of dreams. The growing boy grades his advancing consequence according as he has mounted the "t'gallan" cross-trees, or sat astride the royal yard-arm, or hung his hat upon the truck.‡ Such scenes are schools. Such lessons last for his life and go to character.

Facing about, towards the east and south, the eye followed down the slopes and ever broad, long levels, shading from bright to dark with green home-fields, open wood-lots and uncut forests, until it struck the firm bulwark of the horizon, the noble crowns of the new-named Wrentham Hills, a memory of those left behind, with here and there a broad farm

---

* Kenduskeag Stream flows about 30 miles from the west into Bangor, striking the Penobscot River at a perpendicular angle, providing waterfront space for berths where ships could unload their cargo directly into downtown stores and warehouses.

† The calyx (modern spelling) of a flower is the green part that supports the blossom and from which it emerges. Kenduskeag Stream flows about 30 miles from the west into Bangor, striking the Penobscot River at a perpendicular angle, providing waterfront space for berths where ships could unload their cargo directly into downtown stores and warehouses.

‡ "T'gallan" Topgallant is a sail cloth in the topmost section of the sail on a square-rigged sailing ship. A truck is the rounded top of a mast that helps shed water away from the top and through which the halyards are passed.

clearing, with its clustered home buildings and great barns shining back over forest and field, over hill and dale, from their bastions and terraces eight and ten miles away. Farther and higher yet stand the solitary summits, Peaked Mountain, Black Cap, and Blue Hill, sun-dials of the morning and mid-afternoon.

This bold crest of observation made the frontage of a homestead, four hundred and forty yards on the river, and with a depth of more than a mile and a quarter, a goodly tract, for contemplation or for exercise. About half of this—the eastern and southern slope—was cleared and set in working and bearing order. In due course of events, this tract was divided length-wise, in equal portions, between father and son. This father was Joshua Chamberlain,* scion of an old English and New England family, each generation in its day bearing good hand and name in all the hard fighting done for liberty and light, himself somewhat inclined to be independent, self-reliant, self-commanding; with a possible propensity to command others also; early migrating to Maine, and thence being returned as representative to the General Court of Massachusetts; afterwards a Colonel in the war with England in 1812; court-martialed for disobedience of orders in that when a pusillanimous retreat was ordered at the battle of Hampden, he responded by riding to the front with the astonishing declaration, "There shall not a man leave the ground!"† Exonerated and justified by the Court, he was promoted to command the most advanced outpost of the American Army at Eastport, Maine; revenged upon by the British, who burned at his ship-yard on the Penobscot a new ship just launched and another on the stocks; a loss from which he did not recover, but removed farther up the river to his quiet estate, which in the tradition of Norman descent was named Tankerville, marked like himself with bold front and a high head. A man of much dignity of bearing and of speech, never appearing on the street without high hat, full frock, white neck-tie, and gold-headed cane; a staunch Episcopalian well ordering his household, a chieftain at his board, around which all his family and familiars gathered and stood while he asked

---

* The author's grandfather and namesake. The author's parents named him Lawrence Chamberlain at birth, rather than Joshua Lawrence Chamberlain, III. A few years later, at his mother's request the name Joshua was added as a first name. There is no evidence that he ever used the "III" after his name.

† On September 3, 1813, a small British fleet landed 750 soldiers and several artillery pieces near the present-day town of Hampden, ten miles downriver from Bangor. Reportedly, between 300 and 600 local militia turned out to oppose the British force. Chamberlain's grandfather and namesake, Joshua Lawrence Chamberlain, a major of militia, commanded the left wing of the American force. The entire engagement lasted just twenty minutes, as the Americans fled as soon as the British forces arrived on the field. Major Chamberlain tried, in vain, to rally the panicked and fleeing men but to no avail. Two years later, a court-martial cleared him of any wrongdoing in the fiasco.

the divine blessing, like Saul of old while as yet he inquired of God. A stern man, with his own mind and speaking it; but gentle and loving to his own blood or liking, patient towards the weak, forbearing to abuse advantage, scorning dishonor.

The son was named Joshua also, a favorite name by force of some liking for the old, on-going character that "left nothing undone which the Lord had commanded"; a stalwart, earnest, thoughtful, inward-looking man; of a high order of ability; combining both insight and comprehension; with a deep vein of poetic imagination; claiming no special sanctity, but respecting all sanctities; an old-school theologian; not glorying much in free-will,* but holding himself well in hand and himself trusting all to God, casting all upon Him with an almost desperate throw, content to take his place according to the eternal decrees. Yet withal a man among men solid and square, of deep affections, generous and tender, frank and brave; a hale and hearty companion also, with a quick sense of analogies and incongruities, a good critic and not capable of satire, with a wit and drollery of metaphor which in a single sentence would turn the tables on an antagonist, and extinguish an argument in a general roar of laughter.

On the breaking up of his father's shipyard, ~~he had taken his broad~~ he had manfully shouldered his broadaxe and gone to the St. Croix. Here he found ample opportunity to exercise his previous experience in handling men as well as timber.†

He returned in due time with the reward of many a skilful blow, bought half the homestead, and built on a line with the father's own and at "dignified distance" from it, under the shelter of the crest of the "bank," a modest cottage. Hither he brought for bride a daughter of an old Massachusetts family, a group of which after the revolution had settled among the Wrentham Hills—a town's breadth back from the river—where they held their place and prestige well; comfortable in property, federalists in politics, and Puritan in religion. The bride's mother was Lydia Dupee, a

---

* As the name implies, Free Will Baptists held to the doctrine that God did not control every aspect of their lives but rather allowed humans to determine their own fate through their own actions. During the nineteenth century, there was a substantial presence of Free Will Baptists in Maine, including a significant congregation and church on Essex Street in Bangor.

† The St. Croix River forms the eastern boundary of Maine with Canada seventy miles eastward from Brewer. Lumber operations in those days required a river to transport the logs to sawmills downstream where they were sawn into boards and loaded onto ships. Felling trees with a broadaxe and then dragging them to the riverside via oxen was dangerous work, usually done in winter when the ground was frozen. With the spring melt, the logs would roll into the river and men with cleated shoes would run across the tops of them, driving them downstream to their destination.

decided Huguenot* in blood and temperament, descending through three generations of worthy men, from Jean Dupuis, who came to Boston from Rochelle in France in 1685, a refugee from the cruelties consequent on the Revocation of the Edict of Nantes.† A shapely and beautiful figure was the bride, wonderful in grace and courtesy of manners, with sweetness and vivacity of expression both in face and speech, accustomed to praise and not ignorant of adulation; but holding all her virtues immodesty and equipoise. Much of the French temperament there was within this serious English breeding; so that there must have been an unending conflict between her doubly enforced, rigorous orthodoxy and her joyous freedom of spirit and love of the bright and rich and beautiful. This craving was humored by the young husband, who was proud to see its expression in her apparel and home surroundings. Indeed, on the prospect of her marriage she had made a mysterious visit to Boston, and with a portion of her dowry had purchased such furnishings for her modest little boudoir as had not at that time been seen on either side of the Penobscot. She had, moreover, an irresistible sense of humor. ~~(so that with the chosen company of some young cousins on the mother's side, well-known scenes and characters would be portrayed with such climacteric touches and with such realistic "effects" that an outside listener might deem that these ringing walls were not reaching sounds of merriment, but screams of pain and protest and supplications for very life.)~~ Sometimes, indeed, this mirthful temperament would assert itself at untimely seasons; for there are those who still remember how in somewhat mature years when the requirements of Puritan discipline demanded judicial action, rebuke and chastisement lost half their potency when at some droll plea of the culprit he would see her face turned aside, and her frame convulsed, in a vain effort to maintain "the dignity of the Court." But in and above all, she was a conscientious, faithful, just and judicious woman.

It was a good alliance, this masculine, Norman-English sternness and strength with the brilliancy and joyousness of the South of France. It promised well of a home where not only melody should ring, but ever varying, deep based, high-toned harmony. It was fulfilled in the sequel of the years.

In this home, on a bright September morning in 1828, the natal day of the Virgin Mary, an "undersigned coincidence," and hence powerful proof of something, was born to them a boy. The gallant sea-fight off the

---

* Huguenots were members of the Protestant Reformed Church of France at a time when most of France was overwhelmingly Catholic.

† The 1598 Edict of Nantes granted rights to Protestant Huguenots in largely Catholic France. It was revoked by Louis XIV in 1685, declaring Protestantism illegal. This caused an exodus of hundreds of thousands of Protestants from France and an increase in hostility among France's Protestant neighbors.

New England coast in which the heroic Lawrence mortally stricken, went down with the last ringing order, "Don't give up the ship," had made so lasting an impression on the youthful imagination of the young man that no name would answer for his boy but that of Lawrence.* So it stood, alone, for years, until long afterwards when about to be written on public records, the mother, loyal to her husband's house, wished to prefix, at the sacrifice of her instinct of beauty, that other name, by no means tame in its associations, ancient or modern, Joshua.

The lad grew properly; well guarded and instructed. The sunny slope between the two houses with the beautiful spring mid-way, gave ample field for exercise; while walks along the high crest above the river revealed the margin of a wider world. Private instruction from a sweet young aunt, who among other things tried to develop in him an exceedingly deep-planted and reluctant genius for drawing and coloring, gave sufficient exercise and information for his mental powers. Religious obligations were early inculcated and applied.

An unfortunate uncertainty existed between the doctrines of the Jewish, the Huguenot, and the Puritan religions, as to whether the Sabbath began at the sunset on Saturday evening, or at sunrise on Sunday morning, resulted in giving the question the benefit of the doubt, so that both interpretations being adopted, a period of thirty-six hours was set aside as holy time during which nothing that belonged to this world must be touched or thought of, except matters of life and death, if such can be considered as belonging here. Church and Sunday School were strictly attended. Every omission of a single service of either must be made up for by committing to memory one of the Psalms, an appointed portion of the "Beatitudes," or a hymn from "Watts and Select," and repeating it at the mother's knee before sunset Sunday evening.† In due time, the "Assembly's shorter Catechism" was in like manner recited form cover to cover.‡ Those were not things to smile at then; still less to be smiled at since, or now. For well and fittingly remembered in the after struggles and darkness and temptations of life, as

---

* During the War of 1812, Captain James Lawrence commanded the USS *Chesapeake* against HMS *Shannon*. After being mortally wounded during the battle, he is said to have cried out "Don't give up the ship" as his men carried him below. Lawrence's friend Captain Oliver Hazard Perry heard of Lawrence's actions and raised an ensign to the top of his ship with the famous cry stitched into it.

† Rev. Isaac Watts was a prolific English hymn writer whose works were published in 1707–1709 in the book *Hymns and Spiritual Songs in Three Books*. In 1840 Dr. Samuel Worcester, professor of rhetoric at Amherst College, published a collection of hymns he titled *The Psalms, Hymns, and Spiritual Songs of the Rev. Isaac Watts, D.D. to Which Are Added Select Hymns From Other Authors*. This newer volume became known as "Watts and Select" in contrast to the "Watts, unabridged."

‡ The *Assembly's Shorter Catechism* was originally compiled in 1647, at the height of the English Reformation, so parents and clergy could train their children to be good Protestants.

well as in its joys and triumphs, come back upon the tongue as one's own utterance those strong and soul-supporting messages; and, perchance, riding into the storm of battle, or lying among the lost on the field of carnage, those holy words afloat up in the soul like strains of heavenly music, and then one knows what it means to learn "by heart."

Another great lesson in life came under the "dark disguise" of a new white hat. The thoughtful father, on a spring visit to New York City wishing to bring home some token not only of his remembrance but of the great metropolis, and meaning to serve usual ends and at the same time to gratify the somewhat romantic tastes of his aspiring little family, had selected several articles of fashionable apparel. In the distribution the boy found himself the favored recipient of a white fur hat, a stiff tall hat. A rich and costly hat. Doubtless imported. Very likely the work of distant kinsmen of his among the descendants of some artist-artisan Huguenot who had escaped murder and banishment in Rochelle. But was it a mercy to be wholly thankful for? No doubt duty, discipline, gratitude, good-breeding demanded thanks all around. But however fashionable in France and sought for in New York City, this was by no means certain to be regarded in the Calvinistic and boy-abounding village of Brewer, Maine. Happily it was rather too good a hat for every day. So the ordeal was to be an appurtenance of Sundays and other festive days. The fortunes of this hat is a tale that could be fitly told only by the weird genius of Ossian. The writer of this, distrusting his powers of detailed description, permits himself to substitute for such an attempt some verses suggested by the subject read at a family gathering in honor of the revered father long years after the events herein recorded. A few things only need be added here by way of preface or explanation. This hat was worn successively by each of the four boys as they reached the age of eight—not commonly, but on proper occasions during three or four years probation and privilege, and years after all of them passed through the great experiences, and two had passed also the final one on Earth, the old hat was found carefully placed among sacred relics in the innermost treasure-room of the house. Not long afterward a sudden fire destroyed a portion of the house, a tongue of flame struck into the recesses, and licked the hat in its embrace consuming that utterly, and nothing else.

THE OLD WHITE HAT.

Nothing but an old white hat! Mocking speech men make of that. Pet of fashion; sport of fate;
Sought in love; cast off in hate. But neath this old hat, I deem,

Slumbers yet some deathless dream, O'er whose reaches, still and far,

Broods this mystic, guardian star. Human hearts are passing strange; Over great and
small they range; Lowly things they lift to high; Dying things they let not die.

Question then, this history; Reverent, read this mystery.

In the old home's treasure-room, Deep recessed in golden gloom, Garnered
tokens of the years,

Cherished yet, through smiles and tears, Quaint old things that had their day,
Storied, stored, not put away!

Mother's gift, and childhood's toy; Nose-gay token of the boy; Maiden wreath of
bridal bloom, Breathing still their long perfume; Letters wrapped in laces rare,
Bible marked with tress of hair;

Heart's first gift, and soul's best truth, Lore of love and light of youth,

Of all life has given, or can, Token yet, and talisman.

What is that amidst them all, Silks that tapestry the wall,

O'er the head of hood and gown, Soft and somber, looking down? What a
curious label that!,

"All the boys have worn this hat!" Tall of crown, and scant of brim, Light and
white and sleek and slim, Height of city fashion once,

Fitting crown of dude or dunce,

Filled with lessons parabolic, Scourge to some, to other frolic For round just this
kind of thing Country boys will form a ring And with mocking reverence
greet When encountered on the street.

But one day this hat was bought, 'Twas a favor all unsought,

For a brow most melancholic, Diadem most diabolic.

Then was proved that adage old, Of the great and mighty told,

"Sore the head that wears the crown; Blessed when he lays it down." 'Twas too
good to wear to school; That reversed the holy rule;

Six days rest like that of heaven; Then came one, with devils seven. For to church
this hat to wear Tried the spirit martyrs bear;

And the fight to keep it on

Fierce as those that crowns have won. Oft the wearer lingered late

Hoping thus to baffle fate.

When he slowly reached the church From the door with leer and lurch Swung
some villain lying flat, "Now, by Jove, I'll have that hat!" So tis ever; evil still

Mocks and buffets our good will; In the narrow way and strait Hides some Satan
at the gate, Now the lad, his conflict o'er

Enters trembling the pew door, Take Heed! Ye with haughty eyes, Nor this little
one despise;

For perchance in God's clear sight None so broken and contrite!

Service o'er new zeal to show, Last to come was first to go, Took the benediction
true,

"Peace he sought, and homeward flew. Safe within his room alone

Sat the boy with face of stone;

For high court he now would hold, And give his righteous judgment bold. To the bar he summoned self;

For chief witness that white elf; Jury, all the powers within Scorning cowardice as sin.

Stern the trial, strong the plea, "Take this bitter sup from me!" But with voice and aspect grave

Sentence thus the young judge gave; "Sure this hat was made" he said, To be worn on human head:

Though in my esteem not wise, Good men made it just my size. And the giver, wise though strict Would not willingly afflict;

Nor should e'er a recreant voice Rise against a loving choice.

So 'tis right; and I will dare This in the world's face to wear,

And through all the gibe and jeer Calmly on my course to steer,

Right to seek, and not turn back; White, though all about is black;

High, though compassed round with love I, and this hat, straight will go!

Thence through many a costly fight Sailed the hat, for freedom's right, Gage of war; no flag of truce, Proud midst malice and abuse, Boxed and beat, but not let go; Lowered never to a foe;

But like pennon nailed to mast Standing stiffer in the blast.

So it fared for all the rest; Boyhood's bane was manhood's test. Till from ordeal dread

Came the hat, still high of head; Broken-brimmed and marred at crown, To a halo softened down;

Trophy of the gauntlets run, Wreath of peace we all had won. Solved is now the mystery, Through the heart's deep history. For the Father, evermore, 'Neath that hat sees faces four;

Two, that safely passed death's portal, Bright with youth and truth immortal: Two, still marred by time and strife, Battling up the crests of life.

In his home the father lone, Token keeps of all his own

Guards this hat, so quaint and queer, 'Mong the few things life leaves dear "All the boys have worn this hat."

Yes, good father, mark you that; In life's ordeal great and sore Tried and tested, all we four, Never yet to fear or scorn,

Bent the head this hat had worn. Many a noble deed and bold Wrought our sires days of old; Blazonries in battle won

Passed from father to the son. But no kingly touch or word Like this hat hath rank conferred So the crown and lion still

Mark the crest of Tankerville. 'Twas not meet that such a crown To base use should be cast down, Trodden under foot of men, Moulder back to earth again.

So there came a flame of fire, Not with terror, not with ire, But strong messenger of love

Mightier things than death to prove. Through the house he lightly sprung, Straight
to where the old hat hung; Nothing common touched he there. One sole thing
his sacred care;
Priest-like to be pure he turned, On the altar blessed and burned; Wrought his
ministry of love, Bore the white hat soft above.
Now it knoweth no decay Precious in our sight always, Till the father and we four
Live again the days of yore

A momentous change in the home surroundings followed the return
of the master from a visit to the South. He had been much impressed with
the plantation style of living. Accordingly he shortly built a mansion in
the midst of his largest, level field at the foot of the slope from the river
bank, remote from other houses, and laid out in a large quadrangle for a
home-domain, around which he began at once to bring in a number of
retainers and dependents, these words being taken both in an active and a
passive sense, but all the same most wholly positive. For the retainers were
retained, and the dependents surely depended, but could also be depended
on.

These were chiefly Irish families of various quality and condition. All
were poor, and were favored accordingly. So they were contented and
fairly prosperous in the humble cottages the "master" had built for them.
All, certainly, would have fought for him "the Captain" in truly feudal or
clannish fashion.

[Some, though but coarsely clad and speaking imperfectly our lan=
guage, were made welcome guests in the house and at the table; where they
bore themselves with dignity and often with almost courtly grace, and in
their broken speech showed instincts of the blood and scarcely lost tradi=
tions of a once royal race.]

The river, and the wide panorama from its bank were lost to view.
But fortunately the level field was traversed by a brook. This gave scope for
vigorous developments of boy-engineering.

Bridges, dams, water-wheels and probationary mills bestrode the
stream, taking the capital of the constructors, and trenching no little upon
that of the "landed proprietors" thereabouts. Great was the fun in the
freshet times, when all was swept away, and a chaos of elements and fabrics
came roaring down the brook, swirling around the trunks of the mighty
elms. Then the rallying and rescue; reckless daring and hair's-breadth
escapes; the exhilarating shock of a sudden drenching, and the manly
exploit of working wet clothes dry.

But water is not a necessity for marine experiences. Our lad in the meantime had become chief of a platoon, in which four brothers held a sister in their midst, cherished and guarded like the ark of the covenant. This responsibility he accepted and exercised with, literally, a high hand. For as they, in their course of well administered discipline, became able to climb, he had prepared, under the inspiration of great examples, a tall mast, which he and his crew had cut in the deep woods, and which it required a stout yoke of oxen to draw, and then all hands, by aid of blocks and tackles from the "great beams" of the barn, to raise erect, whereupon he sent up in due order all the spars and rigging practicable, to complete the representation of a ship's foremast. The neighboring rope-walk was laid under charity for stout stays and braces; yards were slung, and caps and cross-trees well secured, for great feats were to be wrought thereon; ox-chains were exalted to the sphere of foot-ropes, while blocks and running rigging were taken by levy or contribution among amused relatives and lenient friends. The mother's apprehensions of broken bones and other marine casualties were quelled by the proffer of useful service through which her carpets might be beaten, and her blankets and sheets well aired, the same being "bent on" in due order as sails. This led to lively times when a refreshing gale would require sudden reefing, or furling, or sending down altogether. Above all was hoisted and flew from sunrise to sunset the American ensign. Common minds of the outside world saw in this only "Launce's color-pole" but the loyal, articled crew heard it with scorn; for to their somewhat strenuous experience it was no less than a "man of war." Ultimately, in token of dignity or defiance, she mounted two guns, trained for either bow. On this exalted instrument were disciplined, developed, tested and approved all the brothers successively, also all relatives who could be lured on board, and all humbler schoolmates who could be impressed into service. The discipline of the ship was stern; the exercise severe.

Especially the duty aloft. The timid and reluctant were clubbed to their stations at various altitudes by the proper officer of the deck. The deserving and enduring were rewarded with rations, which also allured diverse recruits mess time; for a great molasses hogshead with a goodly sediment of sugar was locked up amid-ships, and at stated periods duly opened, at which time also, a sizable tub of doughnuts, a pan of cold sausage or a stack of pumpkin pies would be likely to lend adventitious aid, clandestinely sent round from the abounding kitchen of the house on shore, by the connivance of Huguenot and Irish courtesy and love of fun.

It was mainly fun, then, to be sure; not without a certain suggestion of work; but many who look back upon it from the heat and dust of life are willing to confess that those exercises, developing physical and moral strength, alertness, lightness of limb, sureness of foot and hand, steadiness of eye and nerve, coolness and courage, fortitude and fidelity, voluntary discipline, lifting one a little out of self, all these things learned without the moral disadvantage of real apprenticeship, serve as primary lessons for manhood, and for life.

It must not be thought that in those boyhood days life was all play. There were tasks to be done, duties to be fulfilled. The eldest son in a family of younger children finds many services he can render, both to these and to the parents who do not leave their children to the influences and examples of servants. He is the chief of staff to father and mother. The gauntlet of childhood's diseases has to be run, and happy is he if having passed his ordeal, can serve as nurse or watcher for the rest in turn. He can see that all is right for night in the house or in the stable. He can guard the younger to school, keep a watchful eye over them there, and "lick" the big boys who torment the little ones.

Those were the happy days before the coming of the dreary machine work of the graded schools, where the laws of the factory supplant the laws of the family; where the ruling thought is to economize force and cheapen products; where all moves by mechanics; the children separated by hoppers and sifted by comb-teeth, elevated by cog-wheels and dumped by travelers; where the younger are withdrawn from the elder, and the sister from the brother; where is utterly lost from use all the good that comes from the presence of the more cultivated and more advanced; the learning by contact of others pushing on before them, and showing how each step is taken; reverence for superiority; the inspiration of the vision of actual achievement won by the same road on which each of the others is winning his way as best he can, all free before him, one cannot help feeling that in the new scheme what is gained in quantity is lost in quality.

In those days the boy, taught to look above him, also looks wide around him. In the midst of his duties and relations toward others by the response of some inward chord he finds himself. Then he has his own horizon to fill, some goal to win, some good or goodness to attain. He will make himself fit and worthy for some work and place in life, such as shall be given or achieved. To a thoughtful boy life is already earnest—already real. Blessed boyhood! Heart unstained; choice free; spring-time and seedtime for all that is to be!

Among the genial influences of those school days there was one of more effect than might be foreseen, or fully comprehended at the time. This was the character of the selections in reading books. Heard and read over and over again, these words take deep and abiding hold.

The noble sentiments and ideals familiarized by such collection as that in the "American First Class Book"* have more to do with forming character than much inculcation of trite, didactic rules. Such poems as Bryant's "Green River" and "Waterfowl", have tamed away a turbulent spirit, and strains like "The Apostrophe to Ocean"† and "Marco Bozzaris"‡ have turned the currents of thought away from self and stirred the pulse to nobler ends. A child's mind is moved by more things than we are apt to take into account.

A boy's will is the winds will,
And the thoughts of youth are long, long thoughts.§

There was a thawing sun and a soft south wind one long-ago lingering winter's day in March, and the melting snow-banks shed down their pure waters making a broad pool of bright sea-green in the hollows at their foot. A solitary schoolboy stopped to see wondrous beauty, and stood before it wrapped in thought. The breeze that freshened his brow, the rippling wavelets pressing over towards him, breathed over his spirit from afar some thrilling message known to him alone, and a pure purpose and high resolve were awakened there, which temptation could not touch, nor life let go, nor death dissolve.

Thoughts like these are not unmanly. Nor do they shut a boy up as a dreamer; nor wean him from the world of things. Our lad was among boys. In a not unworthy sense, he was almost an animal among animals. He knew their language; they trusted him, because he trusted them, and kept faith with them.

There were rare secrets in those simple days. Who else in all the world knew where the mysterious night-hawk nested, keeping her secret through very openness and not by craft or cunning, on the bare, flat ledge of the remotest field, she and her brood so like the lichens pressed between her soft, slight body and the sun-steeped rock?

Who else knew the daylight hiding-place of the elusive whippoorwill so dreaded of the household; flitting at evening—invisible form, but incessant, reiterated voice—now seemingly from the lilacs by the doorside, and now from the cherry-tree close under some bed-room window; sending

---

* *The American First Class Book: Or, Exercises in Reading and Recitation* by John Pierpont, 1835.
† From Lord Byron's "Childe Harold's Pilgrimage."
‡ A hero of the 1821 War of Greek Independence, described in a poem by Fitz-Greene Halleck.
§ From "My Lost Youth" by Henry Wadsworth Longfellow, Bowdoin College, class of 1825.

a shiver through hushed hearts, all-helpless, listening to the darkly spoken, inexorable doom or dire sickness or death for some fated loved one there!

But who else could catch the lithe, evasive mare, feeding free in the wide, wild outer pasture, mistress of herself and to be mastered by no man? Vain were it to beguile her with any shallow pan of shaken oats or corn! The unsteady, treacherous eye of her would-be captor would quickly betray itself to her keen inner sense. Behind the outstretched hand proffering these gifts, she sniffed the hempen halter hidden in the other behind the back for her enthrallment. With one disdainful look she would calmly resume her pretended feeding, unbought, unsold!

No more could forty men have caught her with show of force. Did they advance upon her in extended order, thinking to out-flank her and compel surrender by the moral force of the situation? With mane and tail in air like puffs of cannon-smoke she would thunder past them turning their flank in terror and confusion, securing a more commanding position on distant and higher ground. Did they disperse in skirmishing order, or scouting parties, to take her at unawares and cut off her retreat? She would come down like a tornado through Scylla and Charybdis,* scattering her puny environment, for it was not in her philosophy that environment should control her character or condition; and now with a retinue of aroused cattle fired with the contagion of her attitudes and movements, demonstrated to baffled beholder the problems of all the curves known to Conic Sections.† Did they try the methods of plane geometry, and seek to force her to the angle of the corner fence, of which they should form the dense and fatal hypothenuse? With eyes well out on the sides of her head, and ears alert for contingencies on either flank, she stood in silken stillness till some over-confident hand sought to extend the wand of power over her neck, when with one crouching spring and earth-spurning bound she overturned her base, and sent the "hypothenuse" over the fences right and left, launching out—heels front and rear making alternate angles of forty-five degrees in air, and resuming the head of her cattle-cavalcade, tearing down that twenty-acre pasture, which has lost its pastoral aspect, in whirls of marvelous intricacy and completeness, achieving a triumphant solution of that mortal problem which her young friend and sympathizer should have remembered to his advantage in after years, "to find the volume of a

---

* Characters from Homer's *Odyssey*. They were each sea monsters on either side of a narrow strait.

† A curve obtained by intersecting a cone with a plane.

solid produced by the revolution of the 'Cissoid of Diocles'* about a tangent parallel to its diameter."

But who would think that a thirteen-year-old boy could march forth alone, hands swinging frank and free, and manner unconcerned, walk straight up to that indomitable desert-queen, who perchance would come to meet him and rub noses with him, lay one hand upon her shining shoulder, and spring upon her back as if she belonged there? Disdaining the miserable mechanism of saddle or bridle, but at the signal of his old soft hat touching her flank—this serving also for steerage being applied to her port or starboard ear, literally "boxing the compass"† they start off homeward at a speed that suits the mad mood of both. Headlong they come, or as the French so realistically phrase their idiom "ventre a terre,"‡ availing themselves of no gates or bars, but bearing straight for the lowest place on the brush-fence masking a crooked cow-path through the woods. Taking this at a leap, sweeping and swaying through the narrow curves, brushing and ducking under the close overhanging limbs, and at length at a straight run clearing the cow-high bush-fence at a bound, it is only when they strike into the open highway that they are content to take a gait and manner comfortable to the sedate habits of society and the "rules of the road."

The first time this reckless leap in the woods was taken, it involved an incident which had to be made ludicrous to save it from being fatal. Above that "bush-fence" extended the long, elastic branches of a hemlock tree, just high enough to permit a moderate-sized, one-story body to vault the fence underneath and go clear. The mare did not think of this, but the boy did, at least when coming at break-neck speed he caught a glimpse of the impending crisis. There was no means of stopping: it was unsafe to slide off among the sharp stubs and boughs as the mare went over.

This came to pass; or, rather, the mare did: the boy was left hanging, tree-high, like Absalom.§ The mare felt the disencumbered force of the situation, turned round and stood waiting, amused to see her rider coming down out of a tree.

The secret of this sympathy between these two was that they never lied to each other.

---

* Diocles was a Greek mathematician and scholar of geometry who lived from about 240 BC to about 180 BC. He is believed to be the first person to prove the focal property of the parabola. His geometric curve, or "cissoid," solved the mathematical problem of doubling the cube.

† "Boxing the compass" is the action of naming all thirty-two points of the compass in clockwise order.

‡ Literally "belly to the ground" but meaning "at high speed."

§ In 2 Samuel 13:18, Absalom was the third son of David who, after plotting to supplant his father as king, was killed by David's general Joab. This happened when, after riding under a tree, Absalom's hair was caught in the branches leaving him trapped and vulnerable.

One fascinating attraction for Saturday afternoons and occasional holidays was the Indian camps in the deep woods a mile or so beyond the back fields. These Indians were of the Penobscot tribe, which from the earliest times had the reputation of being friendly to the whites. Yet they were so outlandish-looking that it required a little nerve at first to visit their secluded camps. To strangers the "sanups" were inclined to be silent and sullen, and the "squaws" were shy. But they were a well-behaved, good-looking people, after their fashion. The squaws were frequent visitors at the house, where they brought beautiful bead-work of many kinds, moccasins also bead-wrought, and curiously braided and fancy baskets, with the primitive red and blue and now and then a stripe of green, mingled in juxtapositions and contrasts which we are told good taste should not tolerate, all of which found ready sale. On these occasions they dressed in their coquettish best.

Blue was the favorite color for the skirt and loose jacket; but a dash of brilliant red was sure to spangle the neck and bosom, while a low-hanging necklace or cordon of bright tin ornaments, and a stiff, low-crowned, broad-trimmed, Quaker-looking hat over their shining braids of jet-black hair completed a picturesque toilet. The remarkable thing about them was their wonderfully soft, sweet voices.

While the women wore hats, the men wore hoods, or something like the triangular pyramids of blue cloth, or in winter the corner of a gray blanket made into a cowl, the rest of it serving for a befitting cloak.

These camp colloquies were interesting. They had not a wide range of language, and the visitor soon was better adept at Indian than the others were at English. Many were the wild legends told to a wondering half-fearing boy; stories of fierce fights with the Mohawks on the islands of the Penobscot; strange myths of origin and primitive history, or of the sources of the great rivers, in the heart of a far-off mysterious mountain, not a dark and deathly cavern but a vaulted hall resplendent with pure gold and silver and precious stones, where sometimes a dream-driven infatuated Indian, pushing his canoe up the glittering streams, was drawn in and imprisoned in light forever.

The great winter sports were skating and "sliding down hill." For the latter nature provided steep hills everywhere close at hand, where the momentum of the descent would carry half way up the opposite slope, and where for pleasing variety a sharp ridge or artificial bank near the quickest curve of the declivity would give a six- or eight-foot flying leap, that would make a chap lie close, and hold what breath he could, to keep his center of gravity when the craft strikes bottom again. There was one royal course on the main street running from the Holyoke hill down through the village where a well-weighted sled would make a half-mile run. This was too good for boys alone. Good-will and gallantry easily provided means for girls to share the sport. Low-built sleighs were brought, or what were known as "pungs," a light sort of market wagon set on runners, seats taken out and cushions and warm robes and furs put in; a stout sled placed between the shafts in front with a big boy or two in it, hands holding on and heels ready to dig in to steer the craft to right or left. Rosy-cheeked robust girls well bestowed within; pure snow and clear, crisp air without; the twinkling stars above seeming to snap through the sharp atmosphere, and the eyes near by below catching the same flash and tone, this for our side. For the rest, guards and videttes posted on the lower courses and at the intersections of cross-roads, not to protect the coasters, but to warn the villagers and travelers and team-drivers frequenting that thoroughfare, now taken by most "eminent domain." Down we go! Or upward, we know not which: breathless, flying, sinking, soaring; with a sweet delaying at the end, motion quivering to its close, like the tremulous cadence of a song gliding at last to its key-note and resting there in peace.

Endurance to such high joy is, of course, only for those to whom it is given so to enjoy. But the sport is a good one at every grade. It is recreation, invigoration. It teaches the value of good judgment and good steering. One other truth well impressed by this sport is that the level of this earth has a good strong pull on us, and it takes a good strong pull to get away from it. The same law of gravity which rules here appears to have its counterpart in the laws of life, with one remarkable modification. It is quite easy to get to going down hill, and a hard tug to get up. But there is not much fun in sliding down hill in life. The main thing is to keep from it. The fun comes in trying to stay up after you get up; and there is not always much fun in that, either.

As to summer sports, swimming was one. After proper introductory exercises, severer tests were applied: to swim across the river with a twenty-five or thirty pound rock under one arm, and without stopping, turn and swim back with the rock under the other; or if a good crew of boys could be got, to take an old skiff out into mid-river and knock the bottom out of her, and let the boys take care of themselves as best they could, each for himself, if able; but all for each and each for all. This was rather rough sport apparently, but care was taken not to let any reckless and fool-hardy fellow in. Sometimes without fault a mishap was perilously near. The unpleasant experience of seeing from the shore an adventurous young brother come near drowning, sucked by the swift tide current under a big raft, with only a run, a dash, a leap and a plunge, just in season to save him, gave occasion for more specific cautions and vigorous instruction.

Swimming is good both for sport and earnest. It belongs both to the elegant and the useful arts. Besides giving the power to protect one's own life, it often happens, as it did among the experiences herein after recalled, that a good swimmer is able to save a drowning person by a little resolute coolness and nerve.

Gunning was one of the accomplishments of those days. Game abounded and was not too gamey. The fields were broad, but the woods were near. The partridges were plenty in the edges of the clearings, and they stayed with us the year round. The wild pigeons came in flights like clouds and whirlwinds to help gather the grain harvests. It was a beautiful and boy-thrilling sight to see a great flock of them settling down in the top of a big, dead-dry tree at evening-fall for their night's roost, their graceful forms swaying down the branches like the sudden renewal of luxuriant foliage, and their ruddy bosoms thick as they could crowd, reddening deeper with sunset glow. Good for the birds. For many of them their driving up and down the earth was well nigh ended. The temptation to do things on a great scale was irresistible. A famous gun was procured with much bargaining, fully five feet long, and with a bore taking an ounce and a half ball, or a big handful of shot. With "five fingers" of charge in this, there was havoc at both ends. The gun got the habit of kicking and rearing on such occasions. It got on its "high horse." Often after lugging the heavy thing warily a long way round the corner of a wood, creeping among bushes, scrambling through bogs, tearing through briars and thorns, a good sight being drawn on a big flock of birds, the thing was let go, with a bang and a roar and a whir and a whirl, and the three parties to the transaction suddenly separated, the gun end over end backward into the bush; the birds off for undiscovered lands; the boy flat on his back in the grass, thrusting the knuckle of his right fore finger into his mouth and holding on to his right shoulder as if he thought they would get away from him too, the remaining figure of the foreground.

As a purely commercial transaction, the gun business was probably not a success. The income, very likely, did not equal the outlay. The balance of trade was not in favor of the home port. The paternal inspector of customs had occasion to remark upon the huge account for powder and shot footed up at each month's end at the hardware store. The counter-charge for pigeons, partridges and other fowl, not to speak of certain midnight marauders noisome and mephitic that frequented the barn and chicken house, were modestly never presented for audit. The gentle hint was received without a murmur. The gun was exchanged for one less widely destructive of bird and beast and money, with less friction upon muscle and shoulder and domestic peace.

There is one good thing about hunting as a sport. The quantity and intensity of it does not depend on the quality or plenty of the game. In fact, the less game, the more hunting.

Then there are several degrees in this craft. To not a few, the gun is only a sign or password to gain admission to the outer court of the fields or the sanctuary of the woods without subjection to the impertinence or drivel of silly questions as to where you are going and what for. The fools wouldn't know if you were to tell him. But the gun befools them still more. They think they know when they see that, into the wide fields and deep woods, to commune with God's creatures and not to kill them. For who for sport would kill a song-bird? or a bustling familiar squirrel? or a timid, trusting rabbit, sitting up on her haunches with prayerful ears and soft, bright eye wondering if there can be any such thing in this loving world as harm? Not for this; but to lie at length at noontide on the odorous cushion of wilted pine leaves, listening to the innumerable soft sounds, the rustling oaks, the keen-edged whistle of the beeches, the tremulous plaint of the aspen, the Aeolian sighing of the pines; to drink in the multitudinous peace; to dream of the coming years!*

One curious trait of the mind brought to consciousness in those days appeared in a strange sense of relief when after a distracting pursuit of a scattering flock of partridges, some sitting close by on a branch overhead plumb up against the trunk of a tree laughing at you, while you are crouching and creeping and straining, tasking every muscle and every nerve of sensation and of motion, the birds have all outwitted a fellow and finally and definitively disappeared, and you breathe free at last, a certain sense of grave responsibility lifted from the mind. Instead of feeling that you have lost your game, you share in a certain satisfaction they doubtless feel; for they know where they are, and they know where you are, and you don't know either fact, but only that you are free, as they.

Such feeling was, no doubt, a symptom of natural disposition, and intimates, perhaps, a certain weakness of what might be called psychical fibre or energy of will. But it must not be inferred that this feeling existed at all when action was undertaken for others, or in pursuance of a duty. For there was still more strongly marked an almost morbid devotion of will, perfectly and at all hazards, to complete a task or fulfill a trust.

---

* Aeolus was the Greek god of wind.

As these simple incidents are related not for their value in themselves, but as involving concrete illustrations of temperament, or mental constitution according to which character gradually took shape, another example may be given, which carried this suggestion of lack of personal persistence a step farther.

Gunning still accords the physical conditions of the spiritual revelation. It happened one bright winter's day that our lad went out by invitation of another on an expedition of this kind.

Following an old logging road, no unlucky bird or beast thrusting himself upon his fate, the boys were indulging in a friendly chat, when suddenly a strange rare bird flew up and lighted in full sight. It was an excellent moment. Both guns came from the shoulder like a flash, but the boys exchanged a hesitating glance. "Oh let me shoot him!" prays our lad with bated breath—by some strange impulse thinking it necessary to ask permission, but with toss of head and almost scornful puff of nostril, the other boy bangs away, our lad never pulling the trigger. Down comes the bird, a blossom of beauty. In the common admiration over him, our lad who was making up quite a collection of rare specimens, fervent in wish though chastened in will, murmurs a regret that he could not have shot the bird. "Why didn't you do it then? Nobody hindered you" was the cold and rather curt reply, which would be regarded by people of the world a complete answer—a final "settler." So it goes. Self rules. Will wins. World applauds. But was it an answer, after all? It was a curious composite. First, it was itself a question, answered apparently in its own added statement, and so had all the semblance of conclusiveness, like the parliamentary disposition of a resolution passed by a momentary majority by moving a reconsideration and then laying this motion on the table. But to look at this a little further—for a really deep and wide matter of practical life is involved here, the answer was a question, and though put on a trifling occasion, the answer to it reaches into the eternities. "Why" he didn't do it was because there are more things between the Heaven and the Earth than are dreamed of in the questioner's philosophy.

There are many ranges of self and soul. The "why" might be because it is a mean thing to snatch a pleasure at another's loss, even if the rights were equal and no positive wrong were done. And the appendix to the question—"nobody hindered." But somebody did hinder. No body seen or known or recognizable to the propounder, but a body within the body, giving law to both, saying "this pleasure must not be mine," to take it away from another would hurt some higher thing which is still more truly mine.

No more was said; but much was thought, then, and long years after. What could one make of himself in the world with all its competitions, and traffickings and tricks if ruled by such silly thoughts as these? What the good of strength and skill if held in abeyance by reason of thankless rivals and jeering self-seekers? What the use of strenuous will, if neutralized by a scruple of the heart?

But the inquest and remonstrance were vain. The weakness was constitutional. It could not be outgrown. A positive reluctance to seek favors; to take what could be got; to claim what fairly belonged to one by right, became elements of character, and heralded failure in practical affairs which are considered "life." This was not lack of force, but lack of "cheek," nor yet lack of ambition, but rather lack of self-assurance, self-assertion, and that kind of smartness: which too easily stoops to take advantage of the mistakes, the weakness, and the helplessness of others. Is not this to enter life maimed?

But there came a turn of things now that should correct this weakness, and discipline one in audacity and fit him for outside masteries. There was a good military school at Ellsworth, under the charge of Major Whiting of the U.S. Army. This would be a good place for the boy, where he could show what kind of stuff there was in him. Besides there were a few hints now on the double-decked paternal side of the house—quiet colloquies between the father and the grandfather—as to West Point for a destination. So at the age of fourteen he took his place for the "set up drill" before Major Whiting.

One effective way to teach is to demand the impossible. Then a fellow has got to do it. The first wall run up against here was a French language. This was the language of the Institution, for better or for worser—till death do us part. There was a new sense given to the refrain "There's no place like home," for certainly there didn't seem to be any place like it there, unless it should come in, like the Norman conquerors, by way of France. The battering ram to knock down that wall before us was some Frenchman's French Grammar of four hundred and fifty solid pages, out at our service, or we to its. One would gladly have thrown it at or over, any wall ever built by man, rather than try to learn to use it, or to use anything else by or through it. English-moulded Yankee boys to learn French out of a French Grammar written by a Frenchman, a man who couldn't see the subject from an outside point of view, who had never encountered and mastered for himself the peculiar difficulties presented to a foreigner, especially one knowing of the Latin or Romance tongues! It was like penetrating a

Chinese wall without a loophole for fifty miles.* However, we did it. But not without aid. The Major was a strategist. He had made French not only the language of the School, but also of the home, every part of it, from one end to the other. So it was soon found that without that polite language no extra pies and candies could be wheedled out of the kitchen after taps, nor parlor—invitations given on golden evenings to breathe the atmosphere exhaling from that charmed circle, the sweet mistress and the wreath of lily—and rose-cheeked girls who gave that home the beauty and soul of life. So the French Grammar was learned, but after the language.

Other exercises were, of course, the drill, the heavy ordnance, seemingly old King's arms, relics of the grenadiers of the French and Indian wars; marching to church in column of fours, and from the high gallery getting a lofty example of well-doing to the austere aristocrats and fine old families who drank in from faithful Dr. Tenney's† lips the gospel of peace and good-will.

Outside the regular course, and emphatically voluntary, were sundry exercises in the manly art of self-defense, carried on behind closed doors on high walls, but with effects not so well concealed. Certainly in that school we got some notion how to take care of ourselves, and what we were good for, what we could dare and suffer, and do and be.

After that, home again for three eventful, fruitful years. Earnest work, such as a cheerful robust boy could lay hand to. First, the High School in its season, for a final touch to mathematics and surveying; with a dash of Latin; in the winter evening the singing school, and all the year round the farm. It did not take long to gain quite a proficiency as a bass singer. But the great and far-off goal was the "Bass Viol." It was that that dominated both the singing school and the church choir. That was mastery; that was power. The longing prolonged. Bass Viola were high-toned characters in their social habits. They were not to be borrowed by bunglers, nor bought by beggars.

But the Bass Viol could be learned, nevertheless! A good-sized cornstalk answered very well, the places for the strings and the frets for tones and semitones could be cut in at proper distances, and using a smaller stalk for bow, there was no reason why the Bass Viol should not be learned, whatever might be high or low, or near and far. And in the essay, no piercing the nerve-centers of the household. The result was that at the very

---

* Loopholes in a fort or wall are small slits through which those inside can shoot out while exposing the least amount of themselves to return fire.

† Rev. Dr. Sewall Tenney was pastor of the Congregational Church in Ellsworth from 1835 to 1873.

first handling of a veritable Violincello, despite a somewhat rustic style of "bowing," there was no difficulty in playing at sight. Think of the glory of being called out before the whole singing school to take that instrument from the hands of the master, and to be the dictator of time and tine, and to be relied upon as the support and spirit of the grand, on-rushing chorus!

But in the meantime had come heavy reverses upon the generous head of the family. They came through that potent instrumentality of disaster, endorsing notes for others accommodation, an experience so common that one cannot but wonder where the parties can be who profit by these losses, the only parties ever heard of being the losers in the operation. Our father had been largely interested in extensive timber lands, which he had managed very successfully. Now everything was swept away, except the home farm, which, happily was secured to the mother through the kind offices of friends. She was at that time in feeble health, suffering from some disease of the spine which quite disabled her. This disaster coming at such a time seemed to paralyze the father also. He appeared at first to be utterly broken in courage and at a loss which way to turn.

Not so the boy. This was his opportunity. What was he good for, if not for this. He drew the dispirited man out into the sunshine, and astonished him by saying, "Father, you don't know what I can do. This farm ought to carry us. Let me try it. You look about a little. Take another hand at things. Leave the care of the home to me." The effect was remarkable. Little things sometimes lift up the mighty. A harp-strain thrilled to peace the troubled soul of Saul.

There was a double new departure. On the one side recourse to a disused skill in land-surveying, and a later experience in estimating the value of standing timber and timber-lands, in which before long there was ready and extensive employment as expert. On the other, with swelling heart and every pulse aglow, the boy confronts his vast domain and varied responsibility. There was a fine wood-lot not far away which could pay for clearing. At this season of the year, wood would bring quickest return. There was a pair of steers, hardly yet to be called a yoke, which nobody could manage but the one who had brought them up. A big tree could be cut by a not very big man, and split and loaded by aid of alliance with the colonists of Erin, formed on the principles partly of Home Rule but chiefly of the Golden. So the six acres of wood were cut clean, the merchantable portion fairly well marketed, and the rest hauled home to serve for kitchen fires, or bounteously awarded as the share of the faithful helpers. In due season the ground was burnt over and leased out to the same subalterns for planting their potatoes.

Gradually the stumps decayed of the larger ones were uprooted by the aid of the steers, and the former forest worked into a fair and profitable field. It was altogether a successful enterprise, and left a little capital to start out with in the following spring. With this began wide-awake work.

There were several fields, and manifold operations. Planting, ploughing, sowing, hoeing, haying, harvesting, threshing, husking, shelling, housing the fodder, and cellaring the vegetables and root-crops, this was of the nature of hard work, and came to require the enlargement of forces outside and in, and at certain seasons the employment of heavy crews and teams. The father often at home, giving his approving countenance, and at needful times, helping head and hand.

There was labor behind all this, out of that kind which changes curse to blessing; variety, which is said to be the spice of life; and withal, fun, which is its medicine. The younger brothers, Horace, John and Thomas, besides the charge of "the ship," where they kept the colors flying, came in for appointed service according to their strength. The great fireplace in the front kitchen on winter evenings roared its response to the good cheer of songs and games and pantomimes, popping corn and candy-pulling, in which the children took chief part; but all was upon honor, and conducted with dignity and decorum. The youngest brother now drew most attention, being the mother's pet, and hence for mere mischief's sake, an object of pretended jealousy. The second brother, most fertile in fun, kept everything in a rollicking round. Coming suddenly into a room one day where the pet boy and "Jack," the equally indulged big white cat, had been left together a short time, the cat seen scudding under the chairs and sofa; with an altogether limp and crest-fallen appearance, the small boy meanwhile standing stiff and straight in the middle of the floor, a light switch in hand, Horace, the self-appointed minister of justice, leading the family flies to dinner, called out in stern tones, "Thomas, have you been whipping that cat?"— "Wiv' H-how big a stick?" came back the dexterous parry, no falsehood nor prevarication being known to the law of that house, while it was considered by the culprit entirely parliamentary to find some flaw in the indictment whereat one might plead "not guilty."

In the heat of August we usually managed to get a three-weeks outing down the river and on the bay, a habit which acquired wonderful tenacity, and is not wholly given over yet. The sloop "Lapwing" was chartered for that purpose, capable of entertaining quite a company, which this household surely made. It was a glorious experience among the islands of that noble bay, and also put to actual test the seamanship of a self-taught crew, who certainly could not be called "land-lubbers," trained to the royal yard of a man-of-war. The principal experiences were now below, especially when in a stiff squall the lee rail was under and more particularly when grounded on some unknown flats with an ebb tide and a mile away from shore, six or seven good hours presented for exercise of the cogitative faculties, and the evolutions of memory and hope.

On shore, there was much private fun, with a more limited range of actors, but by no means limited variety and scale of action. This was for the most part connected with the peculiar character and performances of the "steers" already mentioned as not entirely civilized. They knew their young master as a friend; but beyond this they had no more confidence in the human race than the "classic" nations of antiquity, who regarded strangers as enemies, and had one name for both, or at any rate gave both meanings to one name. Hence a tendency on both the part of the steers to maintain distances. When free, no stranger could approach them. He could no more yoke them in their yard, then he could wild beasts in their den. This was found rather awkward when increasing work required the service of a "hired man," one Roundy by name. The only way he could yoke them was to coax them into their stalls with tempting food, tie them well up to their stanchions, lug the yoke in, and clap it on them at unawares, and punch the cow-pins in as best he could dodge the horns. To get them out and hitch them to any implement of labor was a war of wits and mechanic skill. The yoked steers were got up into a corner by the tie-up door, the old mare harnessed and backed up just outside, a chain that had somehow surreptitiously been hooked to the yoke-ring from behind, now suddenly snatched through the crack outside and hooked into the whiffle-tree, then throw open the door, start up the mare, and get out of the way! Out they come with an impetus that carries the whole paraphernalia clear across the yard, and mentally impels Roundy to be first at the outer gate. Once hitched to a sled, and fairly got on to a plain road, they were well enough, provided Roundy kept away from them, and nobody appeared ahead. In either such event, they resumed their "natural rights," and took care of themselves.

One day he had gone out with them about a mile into a back wood-lot. In a surprisingly short time, "Buck," the "nigh" one, came galloping home like a buffalo and whisked into his stall, where he knew he would be most free, being most out of sight of his pursuer. Shortly after, the hulking form and yellow head of Roundy hove into view, an ox-bow in one hand and a goad-stick in the other, a marked inequality in the length of his legs giving a droll emphasis to his motion, and on coming within hearing distance a vigorous soliloquy became audible, in which his opinion of the moral character of Buck was unequivocally expressed, the place fixed upon as the final destination of Buck implying a high order of responsible personality to entitle him to that direction. As Roundy himself though a frequent convert, and at such times a loud exhorter, reserved a tenacious belief in the doctrine of "falling from grace" as giving safe room on the lee shore, he certainly should have had more fellow-feeling for poor "Buck," who had sinned only through an esthetic sense of what was not in "keeping," and a resolute determination to be found "at his cost."

Moreover, poor "Bright" was left alone in the woods, holding up the off end of the yoke. Whether Roundy counted on "Bright" coming home in that awkward fashion, or on his leaning the reprobate "Buck" back with his dipping arm across his neck and a loose ox-bow tickling his brisket, deponent saith not. But he concluded it was easier to get "Bright" in, than "Buck" out; and after inordinate absence he reappeared coming down the road, applying the simple mechanic principle of taking "Buck's" place on the nigh side, trying by keeping a little ahead, to palm off on poor "Bright" the fallacy that he had the easiest end of the yoke.

Even in their young friend and master's presence the steers were not always confident of safety. They would keep the furrow very well in plowing until some uncertified stranger approached too near. Then they took the starboard or port tack, straightway. Even with the steady old mare ahead to hold the balance of power, the sudden appearance of a strange visitor would reverse polarities to flight. He was an awe-inspiring, doom-foreboding, holy man. But he had a way, conformable to the Calvinistic theology, of taking to us boys as if we were held in the gall of bitterness and bond of iniquity, and death and Satan had a slight-draft on us. The boys "bent" in a direction like true followers of our august neighbor "Edward Kent." We did not enjoy that; and hence on pastoral visits to the house, if we saw him coming, we availed ourselves of the shortest cut to the back side of the fronded cornfield, where we engaged ourselves in a diligent rehoeing of the outer rows, with such unnamable "iteration" that they took on marvelously excessive growth—the mystery and wonder of the neighborhood. Whether through some prehistoric sympathy, or subtle sense of approaching danger, like that already observed in wild beasts and birds, when these pastoral visits were extended to the fields "Buck" on the nigh side scenting mischief, or fomenting it, would give "Bright" a tip of the horn, whereupon was tumultuously executed a double-quick right wheel, the mare, of course, dragging backward, like an anxious captain seeing that the panting "wheeling flank" scrambles into line; the supposed "commanding officer" following perforce, but finally running the plow—beam-deep, bringing the movement to a halt in good holding ground. It was behooving to go forth and meet the good minister with the peace-offering of apology, and the explanation that these beasts were as mysteriously "possessed" as the swine that ran down into the sea,* and that it was impossible to make them tolerate the presence of anything good. It is not intended to be intimated here that any tedious effort was put forth to battle with the "material-man" instinct of these animals.

As there were no circuses nor minstrel extravagances in those days to keep a due balance of power among the youthful energies, it may be permissible to trouble the memory with one other performance of these allied forces before dismissing them to unjust oblivion. There was a small square field of some two acres to be plowed one Saturday afternoon. It was on high land sloping towards home, half a mile away but unluckily for that occasion, quite within sight, a circumstance to be deprecated to this field the team was anxiously betaken; thoughts, all hand and legs a little sullen under the presentment that there were times coming when solace and civilization, humanity and religion would demand that such hours would be set apart for half-holidays; but secretly cherishing the purpose, long off for them as were the good times coming, to have on their own account, and strictly as private theatricals as good time returning. The plowing is started with double furrows in the middle, so as to one or the side nearest home, and heading that way the turns made square to leave the ground handsome, the plowman holding firmly in hand the guiding lines from the mare's bit, as tiller ropes clamped against the plow-handles, and all moves on orderly, going with a "gee,"† following the sun, as long as it lasted. As the work widened the turns became easier, the plow thus taking a long sweep, did not have to be thrown out of the furrow, and was kept in across the ends. There was at last only a narrow margin of land left, the sun was going down, but our blood in our ratio mounting, a general, instinctive impulse possessed all to wind up in a jubilee which involved a rapid demonstration of the futility of racking our brains with the dull torment of the problem which has murdered mathematicians—"squaring the circle," when it was so much easier to execute the converse and circle the square. A generous slackening of the lines, an inspiriting address to "Buck and Bright" a horn or two of sharp suggestion forward and away bolted the whole caravan; as

---

* Matthew 8:32, "And He said to them, 'Go.' And when they had come out, they went into the herd of swine, and behold, the whole herd of swine ran violently down a steep place into the sea and perished in the waters."

† One of the commands for driving oxen, "gee" means turn right, and is pronounced "jee." The others are "haw" for turn left, "back," "come up" for move forward, "whoa," and "stand."

first one horn and then another the "gee" tending to an "ogee" but all the time rapidly approaching the "apogee." To mix figures it was a billowing gallon, a squall on the port beam, lee rail under, scuppers afloat, main beam dripping, helmsman prone, holding all in hand, but "shaking her" when he can, round crests of the uptorn sod shooting over his shoulder, or he cutting under, everything flying between earth and air.* The land cleared, the plow thrown out and down on its side, without halt, a "bee-line" for home as on wings, and not without buzz and sting. The boy, two legs short of his "forward hands," abandons holding down the plow, springs to the pilot-house of the mare's back, whence he can better steer and control the craft; the plow now striking a hillock and taking earth, then running loose with a bound that reports itself against steers' legs, or even mounting their back, thence passing forward by conduction of electric points of horns, the reaction of iron-shod hoofs ringing against iron hooks and chains and rings again, with the dull "thud" of horn and wood and bone, all charging straight for the barn-yard bars! The bars were up, but so was blood. The father with astonishment and anxiety had seen the whole home-coming flashing like heat-lightning against the evening sky. He came out, and stood, naturally, by the bars, in dread of everything. "Stand clear of the bars," reared the voice from the pilot-house, as the team precipitated itself full tilt against them, the mare rearing and rebounding at the shock, and falling over backwards landing mid-spine upon the yoke and bristling horns, the boy, meanwhile, gliding out from under the imminent impalement, lithe and supple as an eel, fair on his feet, cool and self-assured as if he had done it all with deliberate intent and part of an eternal plan.

The ejaculation of mingled thankfulness, and reproof which the father could not repress, was parried by the exculpation that the steers would come so, and hence the mare must, and that the only way to avert wreck and chaos, of all five, steers and steerer, plow and plowman—was to mount the pilot-house, to hold a perfectly straight course, dead before it, not let her broach to, and let her drive!

There was always enough to do in all weathers. For there were young lambs to care for in the chill March days too sharp for such pink ears and silken fleeces. There were stout calves to be led to suckling which most decidedly led their leaders, reversing the legend of Minos, who by daily lifting young calves is said to have his strength increased step by step with

---

* In sailing parlance, the lee rail of a ship was the one away from the direction of the wind. Scuppers were holes in a vessel's side at the deck level that allowed water to drain off. If the main beam was dripping, the vessel was leaning hard enough for it to be exposed above the waterline, and the lee was rail under water.

the growing weight of his docile charge; but the gymnastics of our calves saw followers but no masters.

There were great piles of wood to split in early spring; and in odd seasons a watchful boy could find many a chance to replenish a slender purse by an outside "job." There was the kind-hearted master of the rope-walk nearby, where a boy would be fairly rewarded for assisting as he could, whether in hatchling hemp, or spinning yarns, or twisting beautiful fish-lines, or "laying" ropes and mighty cables. Here one must be circumspect in motion and apparel; for these fierce revolutionists drag into their deadly embrace every disheveled ragamuffin who comes too near. Better to serve around the great tar-vats and boilers whence pour pungent fumes which are the life-bracing breath drunk in by the primeval pines from a century of suns. There, too, if there is nothing else, there is good Doctor Johnson with his "Anodyne Liniment" only a street away, always glad to have a careful boy come in to help him with his drugs. Here, faint falls of rippling laughter and cultured tones of women's voices from an opposite room woke new impulses of possible things, which would not rest until a daughter of that house had condescended to become private tutor in languages to an aspiring boy. In the spring freshets there was lumber broken adrift, and a stout boy could earn two dollars a day in overhauling rafts if he dared to work while the boards and planks were sinking under him till he was half arm-pit deep in the chilling flood.

There were the brick-yards too, where a boy could do man's work in turning up brick half-dried where they lay in orderly ranks as they had dropped from the moulds. On Saturday afternoons, or before a threatening shower, one could run quickly and be welcome and well-paid to help "hake up" and cover the tender, sun-dried bricks now ready for the kiln. In later seasons and more matured strength there was good demand for work in hauling brick by "the thousand" from the kilns to the vessels at the wharves. This was man's work, with cart and oxen; and the proud test of "relative rank" as a man was to be able to stand in the cart and catch, bare-handed, four bricks at a time thrown none too gently from the side or top of the kiln. Eye and foot and hand must be steady here, for an unready attitude or indecisive catching would have crushed toe for a black mark set against it, the agony of which, boyish pride must not discover, though manhood has more than circumstantial evidence to prove.

In all these works and ways it came to pass that there were no idle hours nor wasted powers nor wholly empty purses in that day of small things.

In speculation, turns were not so fortunate. Two neighboring boys clubbed together and brought a horse for eight dollars. After getting him in good order at some cost of care and money, he would not work in harmony with human plans, and his owners sold him shortly for five dollars; this transaction being faithful witness and truthful prophecy that there are intelligent minds and earnest spirits that cannot learn the tricks of the trade.

But Dudley Johnson fell in the front ranks of the most desperate charge at Chancellorsville, face to the foe; and the cannon-flames that fired the forests and the very field, consuming cannon and cannoneer, left no body of him to be found on Earth, but carried him whole as he was where his footing in the great account will be found well to the fore!*

But the winter must be turned to account for strengthening the finances. That means, for every fellow who thinks he knows enough, teaching school. In this case, the fellow was not very self-assured any way. But it was a necessity on his part, if not equally so for more rural district where they wanted to cheer a teacher who would work cheap and "board round." So a quiet place was found where the father's influence could install a good-sized lad of sixteen. They were honest, sensible, friendly people, among whom the teacher boarded, spending with each family a number of days proportionate to the number of scholars they sent to the school. The district was represented by scholars between the ages of four and twenty-one, from the toddlers whose chubby little legs dangled from the front seats at jumping distance from the floor, to the big boys on the back seats stout and picturesque in their red shirts, and the ruddy robust, wholesome-looking girls in their comfortable, handsome homespun dresses, all right-minded and well-behaved; several of both sides bigger than the master, and probably "smarter." There was no trouble in this school: not enough for healthy action. Everything went too easy. The "master" especially. He was too easy-going; so he easily went. Everybody seemed good; he perhaps tended to be goody-goody. Some of the parents thought he had not "snap" enough, didn't order the boys round enough, didn't make things lively. All this was doubtless true. But he made one positive mistake; he "showed partiality" in the distribution of his calls among the families, and though this was never positively charged, it was doubtless the reason of the School Committee coming in one day and informing him that the school had better close on the next Saturday, after eight weeks session. Here endeth the first lesson. There was not an unkind word spoken.

* Dudley H. Johnson was a lieutenant in Company H of the 17th Maine Infantry Regiment when he was killed in the Battle of Chancellorsville in May 1862. He was two years younger than Joshua Chamberlain.

And the proud father welcomed the son home without reproof, and even managed to find grounds for congratulation. A good stinging reproof was well deserved, but in truth not needed. The boy had shown his "bird" side. He had not learned the life-lesson that it is not enough to do well, but one must make a stir and a fuss about it to attract attention, if he means to get any credit for it. He had not learned that it is necessary to show the power to hurt somebody if he wants to be "anybody."

But wait and see. We'll try that business again. The next winter the boy heard of a school "up river" among the millmen, above Old Town and "above Sundays," where they had broken up every school for three years, and had just pitched the master out of the window while he was at morning prayers, banged the Bible after him, bolted him out and turned the school into pandemonium. This was the place. All that had been gained on the "quarter deck" and the "pilot house" was summoned to the front. A quick run of twenty miles with good sleighing landed a beardless boy and a brown seal-skin trunk at the "Milford Hotel" where the father's character and credit were well known, the School Committee hunted up, the boy examined, approved, engaged! As the Old Testament theology prevailed in that region, there was no "church" on Sunday; but it was a good day to make acquaintances. Manly character there was considered to be something self-respecting, stalwart, square, standing no nonsense, and apt to hit straight out from the shoulder. So after fortifying the spirit with a few extra texts from the "Westminster Catechism" concerning the doctrine of predestination and the final perseverance of the saints, a friendly alliance was sought with the stout stablemen and millmen who rendezvoused at the hotel, and would serve as support of "stretcher-bearers" as the coming action might demand. In the meantime the curious youth of that neighborhood were unaccustomed and somewhat queer capacity of "scholars." They came. The day was devoted to a reconnaissance, evidently on both sides. They all called the teacher "master," and he took occasion to make a few remarks on that text, setting forth the plain truth that this office and title being admitted, carried the necessary inference of certain reciprocal powers and obligations between the parties, and mutual rights and duties, for one common end. He quietly laid on the desk a wand of office well named a "ruler," a stout beech-wood lath as long and handy as a policeman's night-club. Both parties held their courses warily and well until the time of the mid-afternoon recess, when apparently not according to previous custom, the girls were let out first. When they were brought in by appointed signal, the boys then had their turn, which they took with some agitation. At the summons to return, they came in straggling, and lingered round the stove without any necessity from outside temperature. There was evidently mischief breeding. They were made to take their seats as fast as they came, which they did slowly and sullenly, some no doubt from natural inertia, and others disappointed at the non-appearance of their leaders. For three or four of the largest boys, men grown, stayed out ten or fifteen minutes longer than the rest, and when they came in took their station at the stove, chewing a literal as figurative cud, and insolently waited for the master to make the first move. "Take your seats, boys!"—"We want to get warm"—"Go to your seats! You are too warm already!"—"We'll go when we are ready!"—"Go!"—The master's right fist catching the spokesman under the left jaw, on the principle of punishing the offending member, and he went, sidewise, sprawling, over backward at last, and lay motionless, his head against the base-board, ten feet away. The rest, astonished, struck belligerent attitude, but rather on the defensive, while the master edged off towards the desk to get within reach of the "ruler," but bethought himself of trying the effect of sudden command. So with a voice early accustomed to hail the "t'gallan cross-trees," he roared out at them "Pick thet fellow up, and bring him here!" They took a few steps and stood aghast, the fellow lying so still. "Pick him up, I say!" The master himself not a little troubled at the look of things, but knowing it would not do to flat away from the key-note. "Two of you take him up, and carry him home; tell his mother that the master will call and see her after school."—"And you others, attend to your business!"

The rest of the school day was like a funeral. The exercises were perfunctory. It required a little nerve to walk to the boy's home, quite a long road, and nowhere near the "reserves" at the hotel. Rather bolder in face than in fact, he knocked at the door, and was admitted. The boy's head was hurt by stopping too suddenly against the baseboard. He himself was quite subdued. In truth, he behaved like a man. But of course, the "folks" were bound to set up a heavy complaint, and proposed "law." That was a fortunate word. It gave the cue for the defense. "That suits me exactly. 'Law' is just what I'm here for. Now see here. Your people employed me to have this school kept, and are to pay their money and yours for it. Your boy and the others undertook to say we shouldn't do it. It had to be decided in a moment of time whether to let these fellow break up the school, and your own best wishes and interests, and the good name of this community, or to hit this rebellion right in the mouth, at the first word, and save the whole of you." The result was a surprise. "You're right, master. The boy was rightly punished. You'll have no more trouble from him and we guess not from anybody else!" Meantime word had gone to the hotel, and the "master" was escorted in with honors, and the bar-room circle of evening debaters who decided all public questions voted him to be a man. Then he could with dignity and safety show his real concern for the hurt boy. He called in to see him every day until he was able to go back to school. Not a ripple of trouble there any more, and the way was clear for good earnest work.

But the village lacked amusement. What so appropriate to celebrate the new harmony as a singing-school? David wanted a harp, a psaltery and an instrument of ten strings to express his thanksgiving at his deliverance from his friend Saul. The basis of our operations was only the old bass-viol. But one would have thought all the other instruments were here. That school-house never witnessed anything like it. People young and old came from a dozen miles around, and the evenings ended with the triumphant chorus of jingling sleigh-bells. Nobody would hear of the school's closing at the appointed term, and a private subscription was taken up to continue it a month longer. It was a glorious winter, and the memory and friendships of it have in no wise passed away.

THE COLLEGE YEARS

Back, then, to the farm again: home welcome and welcome home! Seventeen years of youth had now passed. Hitherto the motive and plan of action had been to do faithfully and well whatever was at hand to be done. It was time now for positive choices, definite purposes. There had been a tacit agreement in the household to hold that matter in abeyance. Two very distinct lines were sure to be indicated when a decision was demanded. The differences would be radical, resulting from constitution, temperament, and practical tendencies, as already evinced in matters of politics and religion, and in certain cherished ideals. One line would lead to West Point; the other to the Theological Seminary.* We were now at the forks of the road. Resolution must be taken. The main question must now be put. There was only a limited debate. The father favored the Army because it opened a manly, honorable career, and also, no doubt, because his imagination was impressed by the examples and traditions cherished in his youth;† but most of all because there was a chivalrous strain of blood in his composition. The

---

* Bangor, just across the river from the Chamberlain home in Brewer, was home to a theological seminary. The distance between the two was two miles.

† In September 1814, thirty-three years before this time in the narrative, Chamberlain's paternal grandfather and namesake commanded one of the units of local militia in an ill-fated attempt to stop a force of 3,000 British regulars from invading the Bangor area at Hampden during the War of 1812. The American militia line collapsed and fled almost immediately after the British

mother, not without patriotism, and with something of the "chasseur" in her spirit and temper,* did not favor the Army as a "profession." It seemed to her, on the whole, narrowing and enervating. To be a soldier in time of peace presented nothing noble; and to be one in time of war carried some unpleasant suggestions. The ministry was the Lord's own service; and whatever might befall, one would be sure he was faced the right way. The lad himself, now forced to the prominence of a principal party in the case, was not much inclined to either course, for the reason that both alike offered but little scope and freedom. They bound a man by rules and precedents and petty despotisms, and swamped his personality. However, he was willing to please his mother and be a minister, if he could also be a missionary and go to some really heathen country, like Africa or the Pacific islands, where he could take part in civilizing a people and helping them to live right in this world anyway. So the pending question was "laid on the table," and to lose no time while maturing a final judgment it was resolved to stiffen up the sinews by going to college. The boy fixed on Bowdoin, and on entering college with his nineteenth year, only a twelvemonth from the next September. It was a hard pull; there were some things to be done first. The old farm could not be left without greeting and farewell. Many things were to be put in order and prepared. There were seeds to be put in the earth to ripen after he was gone. Part of his heart belonged there.

In another month it was May. Then the soft airs laden with the odor of life, of springing grass and breathing balsams, of bursting buds and wide-winged blossoms angels of the annunciation. And in working season strangely stirring the smell of the renovated earth. Well did they fable it of old that the outwearied athlete recovered strength again the moment he touched the earth.

Warmly the sunshine greets the upturned sod saturated with the sweets of snows. Dear is the companionship of the returning birds following the furrow or singing love songs from the overlooking branches swaying under the burden of the song. Well does the boy with close-cutting scythe know how to spare the sparrow's nest, staking around it a little tuft of uncut grass to guard its peace, if not its privacy. Skilful is he also to avoid the lowly nest of bumblebee, nurse and life carrier to the clover whose blossoms are in turn his sustenance. And so furnished with the instinct and the stinging

---

arrived on the field. Major Joshua L. Chamberlain was acquitted of responsibility at court-martial sometime later.

    ★ *Chasseurs*, literally translated as "hunters," were French light infantry and cavalry soldiers first organized during the War of Austrian Succession in 1743. By 1788 there were about a dozen such units in the French army.

sword to defend his person, and perpetuate the beautiful balance of their mutual life. Peace with the bumblebee, for without him no clover.

But the ever remembered glory of that summer's work was the sowing with grain and "laying down to grass" of a dear old familiar field. The furrows well cross-plowed and harrowed down, leaving the natural slopes like a smooth ground-swell of ocean. It was remote field, a gentle hill-side stooping towards the west, and over the low banks of the brook commanding a view of the city across the river. To have all closed and calm by Sunday this work must be finished Saturday afternoon. One would gladly be alone in such a service, when a field that had been associated with many works of youthful years to come. To a thoughtful spirit sowing is a solemn, caring trustful service. It is communion with all the forces of the Universe, the powers of darkness and of light: gravities, attractions, affinities, upstrivings to the sun: emblem of faith and hope and immortality: burial, resurrection, life renewed forever more.

Turning and returning, measuring the ground carefully with the eye, scattering the precious grain with three casts of the full hand at every step, looking downward, upward, inward! But the scattered seeds must be covered betimes. In this case the light harrowing was followed by the smoothing bush-drag, improvised in the lack of a roller. A fence-post answered well for this, five fair-sized birches, the butts wedged into the mortises and the brush spreading out with sweep behind, the spicy smell of the crushed young leaves freshening the senses. Now in the declining day of the sower, guiding the faithful, knowing mare, companion of his youthful toils, traverses breadth by breadth the field, the figures standing out against the shadows luminous in the sunset glow which has touched the mists above the city across the river with wondrous glory, and thus, all bathed in a golden dream, tenderly pressing that precious earth, for the last time of the dear old times!

But oh! The haying in "Mother's Meadow"! Holiday harvest! Immortal memory! After the hard work of the heated fields was done, off here for a week, encompassed by the deep shade of the circling woods, amidst the sweet wildgrasses by the brookside! The meadow was the work of busy beavers, who had dammed the brook to make themselves a commodious home, the walls still visible where with sagacious eye and sharp tooth they had felled the trees, and well banked and plastered the earth against them with the effective implement at the other extremity of their bodies. All broken now, their wise and goodly work, like their own reign and race. Man had hunted down the cunning life, and the waters had then their way. But not wholly. The beavers shall mark the meadow's bound, and the brook sinking from its ancient bed shall take its meandering course from the levels they had laid, and so follow their behest forever. Light, winged elm-seeds had found good holding in the soft mould of the meadow, and drinking rich nutriment from the congenial soil and air, had grown to magnificent shape and stature, and their wide-spread drooping branches half canopied the scene. Around were thick, deep, dark woods, walling out the bitter winter winds, and framing into a picture of living green the waving summer grasses. Towering above the common woods, and scattered far over the plains, were the gigantic trunks of primeval pines, deadened and stripped to shafts by sweeping fires, save where now and then an unconquerable, branching top uplifted its cross-like standard against the sky, making place for the eagles nests, where fortified by stockade and abbatis,* and defended by beak and talon they reared their young unhurt by any earthly hand.

Ring! go the scythes at sunrise through the tall grasses softened by the night dews. High tossed on nimble forks by the thick flakes, scattered and spread to dry in the noon-tide sun. Raked towards nightfall are under the brooding darkness. Turned and spread again on the morrow, yielding back to air the moisture they drank from earth, and working in their very core the mystic chemistry of sunshine from another world; rolled in great heaps and piled up in cones at evening, standing in rank and order under the misty moon-light like a mighty host encamped. And then the fragrance of the night; the woods, the distilling grasses, the waters, the very earth of the meadow bottom. Is that perfume of the body or of the soul?

And is it now a memory of the mind, or is it imperishable part and parcel of the things themselves?

The hay cannot be moved away in harvesting time; the roads are rough, and the ground too soft for loads like these. So it must be piled up in mighty stacks to await the smooth pavement of the snows, and the firm bridges of the ice, abiding there like the pyramids, silent and long forsaken.

But what of the night-watches during that sojourn in the bosom of the forest? Camped in the recesses of the woods, looking out over the misty meadow, seeming so lone and so far, and up into the infinite sky so full, so near; sheltered by the overspreading branches mighty trees stretched on soft and odorous beds the tender sprays of hemlock and balsam, a great fire of pine knots burning red at your feet, the leaping flames weaving a thousand weird and dancing forms among the shadowy branches, the blue smoke curling away in wreaths and drunk up in gloom; the sparks mounting

---

* *Abbatis* is a French word describing a military barrier formed by laying a log horizontally and fastening pointed sticks to it, directed outward to thwart attack by enemy infantry or cavalry. They were commonly used during the Siege of Petersburg, Virginia, in the last year of the Civil War.

upward till they mingle with the stars, do you sleep, or do you more deeply awaken? Is it here, or elsewhere, your rest?

But that season's work brought also one timely lesson for him about to enter on new and untried tasks, a lesson simple and homely but good for that time and for all time. It was in the haying season. We were in the swale of the brook-field loading hay; the boy forward, driving and pitching; the father following, gathering and raking after. In crossing the brook the hind wheels were just in the bed of the stream when one of the forward Wheels got wedged in between two good-sized stumps, which the driver should have avoided. The team couldn't move. There were only three or four hundred pounds of hay on, but the thing was a dead lock, front and rear. "Clear that wheel," came an imperious voice from across the brook.

Evidently the father did not understand the situation. The affair was a little complicated. "How am I going to do it?" returned the boy, not in inquiry but expostulation, believing the case required consultation, and combination of effort. "Do it; that's how!" rang back the stem bugle-note. Perhaps the underlying thought was to "haw the cattle to," back out the wheel, and straddle the stump. But the terms and tone gave no instructions—only the order. The youth (boy-fool-like, was "mad". He) seized the hub, lifted the wheel clear of the stump, and threw it over with such force that the cart-tongue knocked against the nose of the "off ox" and the whole team was "off" in a jiffy. There was moment's pale astonishment, but not a word was said. There was no "loose talk" allowed around those headquarters, and that text needed no commentary: "Do it! That's how!" There was a maxim whose value far exceeded the occasion. The solution of a thousand problems. An order of action for life, worth infinitely more than worn-out volumes of lifeless learning and years of thumb-sucking irresolution.

Sometimes for companionship and possible service the boy had been taken by his father on some of his timberland surveys and explorations. This was at any rate a good way to learn how to "camp out." Considerable experience of this gave him the right to be looked upon as an expert.

For this reason he was invited to be the junior member of a party consisting of three ministers and two laymen, the latter ministering not a little to the human needs of the party, who undertook to visit Mount Katahdin, the highest mountain in Maine, being only a few feet less in height than Mount Washington in the White Mountains. Leaving civilization at the town of Patten, about a hundred miles above Bangor, the party packed most of the baggage on what had been a horse but now appeared to be a dromedary,* and started by an old winter logging road too rough for any vehicle on wheels, making their first night's camp on the bank of the Branch of the Penobscot below the entrance of the Seboeis River. From this point it was necessary to send the horse back, and distribute the burden among the party. This had to be done on religious rather than equitable principles, the bearing of another's burdens, as those least willing to carry required the most paraphernalia. Some old bateaux† were found to effect the crossing of the river, and from that point the course was laid by compass, and the trail made was marked by "spotting trees," to guide on the way home. But what was the vexation to find at about noon another very positive and particularly negative stream confronting, no less than the wild Wassattaquoik. This, the lighter-bodied of the party would have no difficulty in fording, taking over also much of the cumbrous outfit borne high above the head. A good doctor of divinity, however, though the attraction to the center of the earth held him thitherward with the force of some two hundred pounds, being no Baptist, wouldn't take water, lest he should be carried away.‡ It took a good hour to get together the material for a raft, fortunately favored by a spring freshet which had stranded four or five logs from some lumberman's "drive," a second tier of smaller stuff being laid crosswise on top of these, and yet a third above the latter lengthwise, and a foundation was therefore made for the doctor's faith, in something that would overcome his attraction for earth and his distaste for water. The "goods" being thus transported to another territory, and the raft moored to the bank for service on return, the course was laid and the second camp made on the north bank of Katahdin Pond, a beautiful sheet of clear bright water, well up the foothills of the mountain. It is needless to search a cookbook to find what would make a good supper or breakfast for that occasion, any sort of a hook and the most unscientific bait being all that was requisite by wading out a little into the pond to take in even more than one wanted of those superb lake trout that crowded about one's legs, till he began to doubt which would be the game and which the "keeper." And for a broiler what is better than a forked stick, held before a bed of coals? The next morning early the real ascent began. It was a glorious sight when

---

* A one-humped camel.

† A common river vessel in Maine, a bateau was a rowboat, pointed at bow and stern, used to convey goods, equipment, and other burdens. Sometimes referred to as the "white man's canoe" it served a purpose similar to that of the Native American birchbark canoe. It was not uncommon to find one or both types of these vessels in the woods or brush at popular river crossings.

‡ The reference to Baptists has to do with their practice of baptizing by immersion in water rather than the sprinkling of it on the forehead of those being baptized.

working well up the southern "slide," the innumerable streams and lakes came to view, threading and gemming the far-stretching woods, their places marked by light wreaths of mist drawn up by rays of the ascending sun into airy lakes, and weaving a vast network of heavenly tracery between the dark forests and the clear blue sky, that made the backward look in the welcome pauses of the toilsome climbing too tempting for any other devotion, however duty demanded and destination allured. Indeed the main body of the party were fain to linger around their place of "nooning" on the crest of the marvelous "crater" that forms the interior heart of the mountain, while these sky-bastions thrown up and out make the shining walls that glitter snow-like from afar ~~against the northern sky~~.*

All the distant scene spoke the living glories of the earth and sky. All the near spoke the desolation of solitary power. Fragments of rock, shattered and splintered by elemental storms; boulders strewn as if hurled in the titan-sport of unearthly armies; great barren slides where a commanding voice had spoken, bidding the mountain to remove and be cast into the midst of the sea; all, the peace of death, save where the wondrous lichens and curious snow-plants and rare alpine flowers had caught a ray of sunshine into their tiny hearts, and reflected back the tones of the infinite heaven: no breath of life save of some curious atom of a bird, wandering there no one knows why but he and God, but with still up-soaring wings to tell the story of the sky.

But two of our adventurers determined to climb the topmost shaft that shot up so bald and sheer that it was called "The Chimney." This was sailor business, this "shinning," but it was achieved; and the younger, after long and fertile expedients, succeeded in breaking off the very pinnacle, a coarse iron-stained granite cone, weighing some seven or eight pounds, which he afterwards carried on his back forty miles, and then took home for trophy and memorial.

Near the lake-side on the lower spur was made a Sunday camp, where the good doctor, in token of hard work done to get up a comfortable camp with plenty of firewood, preached a sermon on the text, "A man was famous as he had lifted up axes against the thick trees."

The party returned on their trail, with no further incident worth recording except the manifestations of beasts—great lovers of the luscious blackberries, which in the crisp, ripe September sunshine tempted the bears

---

* Interestingly, the described events are quite similar to many such expeditions on Katahdin that a young Teddy Roosevelt took part in during his late teens with two local woodsmen. Roosevelt later credited the two men and the rugged Maine landscape with making him both a man and a conservationist.

as well as their more favored rivals, who didn't have to keep so many feet upon the ground.

We parted at the journey's end. All that met and parted there, except the writer, have, after faithful well-doing here, climbed higher yet, and to them are vouchsafed more glorious visions from the mountains of God.

But straightway now came occasion to put all good into practice. There was a heavy task on hand and a steep hill ahead. Those stern requirements of Bowdoin must be met. The inexorable hour would strike: the boy must answer "Here!" It was only twelve months away. He hadn't done much bearing on the college "fit," except in mathematics. He had "read" Virgil at the home academies and high-schools; but knew little of Virgil and less of Latin. Greek was an unknown world. Here was three year's work and one year to do it in. It was "forward" now. No possibility of going back to learn the rudiments of Latin; Caesar, Sallust and Cicero must be conquered by surprise. But he found an ardent armor-bearer in William Hyde.* A Bowdoin man, who not only bore his shield but carried him on it at last into his old College. For Greek, the path was new but clear, and also steep. He was fortunate in this; for he found for tutor Lemon Bennett, a Waterville man, who after the stern example of that virile old-school discipline, made him pass his initiation by committing to memory and reciting *verbatim* the whole of Kühner's Unabridged Greek Grammar from alpha to omega. Then Homer, Herodotus and Thucydides came to look in on us like old friends. The arena for this race-horse training was the floor of the famous backward-boy "Chatham University," appropriately occupying the spacious stable-loft in General Steven's barn, protected from the power of unclean spirits by the proximity of Bangor Theological Seminary, just across the street. To this trial-ground the youthful candidate marched every day, a mile and a quarter, at ten o'clock, to "recite his lessons," and receive casual hints of instruction. Three hours of this and then home, for a new stretch.

This tasking course was kept up and conducted in strict accordance with a rigid written schedule nailed to the bookcase door, in which every hour of the day, from 5 a.m. to 10 p.m., was inexorably appropriated. For perfect seclusion and self-command the youthful devotee had "finished off" an ample room in the spacious garret of the home, one window looking at the beckoning sunset sky and the other at the north star around which the whole heaven rolls. These were his lights and his chief companions. Good

---

* William Lyman Hyde (Bowdoin, class of 1842) originally of Bath, Maine, taught in Ellsworth from 1842 to 1845, and at the Bangor Theological Seminary in 1848, the year this portion of the story describes.

exercise was provided in winter by preparing and carrying up his own fire-wood. There is no muscle-making, man-building exercise in all the jockeying tricks and scientific gymnastics of modern "scholarship" to compare with splitting wood, especially when this is yellow birch and rock maple. Every muscle and tissue of the body from scalp to little toe is worked into play. Calisthenics may teach how to grow in grace, but to pack brawn into the shoulders and strength into the back and loins and give litheness and suppleness to every joint and limb, try the battle-axe of Coeur de Leon on a rock maple butt.

A delight for summer's variety, and a god-send for sympathetic interest and good fellowship, was the father's coming up to the open garret to give lessons and practice in broadsword exercise. Avoided head-splitting is as good experience as achieved wood-splitting. This sport grew so serious at last that by mutual consent, and with mutual respect, not unmingled with a proper and personal fear, each for the other, professedly, the foils and sticks were dropped, and a treaty of "perpetual peace" concluded, far deeper, in intent and content, than those promulgated under this well-worn phrase by crafty nations that have lost their hoped-for advantage and conclude to watch each other's weakness and their own opportunity.

But thoughtfulness deepened upon the spirit of the boy, as he now confronted life and all its reaches. The teachings that surrounded his early years, the drawings of a religious nature and the need of saving grace and a loving, divine brotherhood led him to seek the earthly communion of those who were striving to follow the law of Christ. Although unable to present an experience like that of desperate sinners and sudden saints, he was still accepted by the loving circle under whose influence he had been reared, and so admitted to the Congregational Church of Brewer, the mother church of all the region far around. In this communion he found strength and growth, while toiling forward to the appointed goal.

This time came all too soon—the opening of the College year. Our candidate was not more than half ready. But the college had its long vacation in winter, in those days. Here came a forlorn hope. Would it be possible to bring up this heavy arrearage, and also overtake the College class at the beginning of its second term? It would take a good deal of wood splitting and head splitting to stand up and carry that. At the best one would enter with a poor fit, and then drag along at the foot of the class. Would it not be better to take another year for it? To get all ready, to enter well prepared, and have everything easy? But no! It was now or never. It is just as well to make things ready as to wait till they came round so themselves. There were two things favorable. The first Freshman term is not devoted to getting over ground rapidly, not scholastically, at any rate. It takes all of that term to get the odd and obstinate "fits" together, and to bring the class into compact and even order. Herbert Spencer had not then demonstrated that progress consists in movement from the homogeneous to the heterogeneous. Such a class could advance only as fast as the slowest, and not the fastest. Here was one good chance if a fellow was in live earnest. Then, there was the long winter vacation. Yes! The thing could be done. It only needed a six-month's turn at the right and left "moulinet" to say it should be.

Therefore, in February 1848, William L. Hyde in a sleigh, with a big wooden trunk lashed on behind and the faithful mare ahead, took a green and pale-looking lad into his charge and started by the "shore line," avoiding the "Dixmont Hills" sounding the way along through the deep snow-drifts and "making the buoys on the port hand," Belfast, Rockland, Wiscasset, Bath—keeping these seaports on the left, which would surely lead to the classic haven Brunswick, they anchored there in peace under the second rising sun. Chewing his cap-strings, and confused with mingled sensations of awe and awkwardness, the trembling neophyte was led into the presence of the several professors, examined out of special favor, and by some time in the dead of night, admitted, conditioned only in Sallust's *Jugurtha*. He had expected juggernaut. He was requested to appear with the freshman class at six o'clock the next morning, while as yet nothing earthly could be clearly discerned, with the "works" of one Titus Livy under his arm, and as many of his words as could be absorbed, into the somewhat obfuscated "gray matter" of a throbbing brain.

He had been told, in an unsympathetic, perfunctory manner, that to find his class he should enter at the south door of a big, gloomy building called on the catalogue Winthrop Hall, albeit known to and by the participants and observers of its exercises, under the better descriptive title—"Sodom." Coming out of Chapel in the misty twilight of the morning, he found himself preceded by yawning, motley crowds which were gradually absorbed in the protoplasmic walls of sundry, looming, fog-banks of buildings, and following along by force of suction, instinctively assuming for classmates the greenest looking fellows he could see, and in his loneliness longing for shelter or oblivion, he darted in after them to the first "south door," which he saw closed upon him by those who had entered. He seemed to have left all hope behind! But pushing in, he confronted a dismal bank of jagged faces surrounded by blackened walls, looking for all the world like so many galley-slaves at their benches, but in "dead" reality awaiting sentence on some obliquity in "Smyth's Infinitesimal Calculus," a special incarnation of "the most wonderful instrument ever conceived by man." There was blank astonishment all around. A dazed face stares at the intruder, a nervous hand convulsively shakes the lapel of a threadbare coat, and gasping lips automatically phrase forth the aphorism, "You will find your place at the corresponding door of the next building." Not a guy nor a jeer from a man in that room! That is the reason why they have become ministers, missionaries, judges and generals, and all the things a boy wants to be, and a man wishes he had not been! The latecomer was installed in his own classroom at last, exercises being suspended while he was seated. In due time he was able to stand up and hear Professor Upham read his Livy to him and pronounce it "very good": and the evening and the morning were the first day.

Yes; the mare had done it. Not knowing all she did, faithful to the end whereto she was made to minister. The boy knew, but too well. For once at last, the bond of sympathy was broken.

Unknowing, she had borne him away from all that had been theirs together;—from the wild, unbridled racings over the rough back fields; from the reckless cuts at full speed through the labyrinthine woods: from the flying leaps over the high brush fences, and the conspiring scurry home; from the gallant, shining plow, and the sweet breath of the slow-coming, ruminant steers and the incense of the uplifted earth touched by the uprisen sun; away forever from the shadowy, home-returning pathways, where at evening the song-thrush from the pinnacle of the fir tree above the gathering darkness, with his thrilling triplets summons earth to sky, and sense to soul!

There were depths now opening which her wise instincts could not fathom, courses her fearless affection could not follow. She must, all unknowing, leave him alone to face those fields where one must sow in tears that he may reap in joy; where ashes to ashes, dust to dust, and life for life must be given, so that life may be unto life. What, then, were the communions when at the parting of the morrow, these two drew together, and the boy with things unspeakable in his heart, patted the silken whirlpool on her shining neck, whispered into those sensitive ears thoughts they could not hear, and gazed into those luminous, dark eyes mirroring depths which neither knew!

Before the next night our probationer was assigned to a room in College, on the fourth floor of Maine Hall; for the saving in expense joining with a roommate, George L. Hayes of Rochester, N.H., a manly clean fellow, self-willed but chivalrous.* He was welcomed by classmates. The

---

* Hayes became a lawyer in Russellville, Kentucky, but died in 1854, three years after he graduated from Bowdoin.

sophomores probably thought he was too meek to need "hazing," although his roommate informed him that, owing to his defiant manner, they had taken him out one night in the term before, and tied a rope about his middle and run him up to the top of a pine tree, in an environment of highly insufficient clothing, where they left him to make his way down by quadrumanial methods.* Out of respect for traditional forms a "visitation" was made upon the newcomer, in which, under the guise of solicitous regard for his health, the doors and windows were carefully closed, and pipes of peace were smoked until the lamp looked like a red moon in a foggy night, with the intent to "smoke out" the freshman. But a hint had been given him, and his courtesy and his endurance exceeded the standard of his hosts in the ratio of one sound survivor to twenty early missing and five left disabled on the field.

All went fairly well. But the terrible strain of the past 18 months had left the boy barely strength enough to keep up with his class. In due course came that great epoch in life, the final freshman examinations. Everything was brought up square; the laggard was abreast with his class, with a clean sophomore ticket. Now for triumphant home-returning; great welcome and great rest, fairly earned and woefully needed.

Sophomore year found him a well-seasoned collegian, his place established, his friends chosen, his name known. The boys called him "Jack," which argued well for his good sense and their good nature, for this meant he had made them like him. He had entered his full name on the College records, and there was a new responsibility upon him. He had three names to take care of, the scriptural, the medieval, and the modern. He looked himself over, looked himself through (as well as he could?) and found his weaknesses. First he saw that he was not strong in mathematics, ~~whether~~ by nature, or lack of training. He resolved therefore absolutely to master the mathematical course, severe as it was then to the glory of the College, whether he mastered anything else or not. And as we are not here following chronological lines, but grouping matters under characteristic centers, it may as well be said now that this course was mastered, although at some bleak points he stood alone. For it pleased Professor Smyth[†] to prepare a series of "works," entirely well so denominated, following exactly our successive years with the advancing series of his labors. The result was that this class had the great honor of being the "dummies"—often well-deserving also this designation—on which he practiced his problems to discover their

---

* By use of four "hands" or, in this case, hands and feet.
† Professor William Smyth taught mathematics at Bowdoin from 1824 to 1868.

applicability to human conditions, and the power of the finite mind to drink in and contain the infinite and inconceivable. Well remembered are those weary nights when some problem would be given out for the next morning's demonstration, over which a pale student had sat staring at the words, without moving except to seek some possible kindly hint from the fixed stars which alone had any experience of such things, until those stars were lost in the flush of dawn, before one flush of light would dawn on him as to what the thing was any way, and what way there was to get to know the thing when he saw it. And did the sun ever rise on any such Triumph as shone on that boy's face since Kepler grasped the order of the universe and cried out "O God, I read thy thoughts after Thee!"

But other things came to be thought of as that year rolling on, rolled upward the mockeries, the contradictions, the perils, the possibilities of life. It was necessary to know one's self; to make the supreme choice; to set the compass; and to set the equal resolution which way to go!

There may be those who think this was not difficult, that when the right and the wrong are distinctly presented, it is easy to choose, and having chosen, to hold fast. But the question does not always so present itself before the tumultuous assembly of cravings and impulses that form the judicial tribunal of the age of twenty years. The trouble is that the right and wrong do not express their counterpart in what appears as the good and the evil; certainly they are not again reflected in what we know as pleasure and pain. Philosophers may argue and dictate as they will; no process, either logical or practical, will lead back through this series from the latter to the former: no subtle chemistry can resolve the one into the other: the beating heart does not trust itself to solve the problem, from the known to find the unknown, from the life to find the law. "Be virtuous and you will be happy" is the sublime mandate of the copy-books; but the way is long; the path is steep. The goal is found only on the far, higher pinnacles of life. Rather should one say, "Be virtuous and you shall pass through pain, and suffer evil, but at the end of the grievous passage you shall find the good." No: to see is not to follow; to know is not to do.

Believe, then, it is not so easy when the clear beam of light in the soul is for its earliest utterance but a dizzying whirl, a phantasmagory of broken colors, wisely to choose the right. Nor, indeed, is this always virtue; for such is sometimes adopted as a rule though cold and calculating ambition to gain selfish advantage. But to a manly, generous heart, when the blood runs full and warm, when the dizzying tremor floats the senses into a delicious dream, or the throbbing pulse of abounding strength pushes out like nature in luxuriance and overflow of life, or storm of energy, to free, high-hearted, chivalrous, wild tourney of sense and soul, not basely betraying high to low, not using this effluence of divine powers and gifts to make one's self a beast, but to become a God, this, gentlemen and ladies of the jury, this is temptation. One must, then, bring the distant nearer than the near. He must look away from the confusions and beguilements of beginnings to the consummate whole unto whose needs and masteries these things were preconfigured; he must rise to the heights of life, which means, in truth, to withdraw within the consciousness of nature's true nobility, the supremacy of the spiritual over the material, and hence the transmutation of the material into the spiritual, which is the mystery and glory of life; the redemption of flesh through spirit, of body through soul.

Then one can set his compass, and fix his resolve, "I will be worthy of what is best in me, hold myself ready for what is noblest in doing or suffering as the years of God unfold.

> "As the bird wings and sings Let us cry, all good things
> Are ours; nor soul helps flesh more now Than flesh helps soul."

To hold a comfortable immunity from annoyance in taking a peculiar stand it is sometimes necessary to appear narrow, if not prudish. So here no "good-fellowship" nor entreaty, nor temptation could induce our young student to drink so much as a glass of cider in College, however freely he might do so at home. The line once broken, he would be subjected to the necessity of endless explanations and apologies. The burden of proof would be on him to show cause why he should not treat one friend like another, and so go on drinking, deepening his experience in quantity and quality. But his law once laid down, without putting on superior airs, but firmly, it was treated with perfect respect, and saved him from a world of trouble.

Nor did he feel like an unwelcome guest at class suppers because someone would interpose at a critical moment with the injunction "O, boys we can't tell that story now; Jack is here." This did not seem to throw any chill on the festivities nor was that the least of College honors.

But the innocent do not always escape. In the early summer came that holiday outing known as "class-tree day," the favor being granted, or executed, to approve the custom of each class planting a tree in the border of the College grounds. Of course the tree was sought as far as possible from the College, and also from the town, for reasons which may become obvious. On this occasion the tree was sought and found in the town of Lisbon, some 10 miles away. A two-horse hayrick was well loaded with this prize and arboreal bearings and the party convoying it, the latter also somewhat weighted with the "refreshments" freely partaken of during the day, the remnants of which, including some private stores in "watertight compartments," furnished means for renewed, transmuted strength after starting for "home." The result was that, although adopting the rather contradictory policy of taking a circuitous route through the country and the shortest cuts through towns, the whirls round sharp corners and collisions with carts and dogs and boys, and the hilarious and aggravating answers returned to protests of sober citizens attracted the very adverse attention it was desired to avoid, so that complaints reached the faculty. Arrival was achieved at night, and the tree was forthwith planted, lest the "sun should strike the roots" and also to avoid objective observation in the case of subjective ones in the dark and to secure the aid of the "great dipper" in trying to plumb the trunk. The next morning began the "summoning," and the results being meager, at about noon "Chamberlain" was sent for to go to the President's house about a mile down town. Those of the previous party who were not "unwell" assembled in his room to hold a conference, sympathizing with the predicament of one who had vainly rebuked the misdemeanors and yet had the final brunt fall on him; and who moreover would neither lie about the affair nor expose the guilty parties. They wanted to know what he was going to do. "I shall bear the punishment, whatever it may be." They didn't quite like that, but proposed to wait and see what would happen, confident that Jack wouldn't "give them away," anyhow.

The president was august and bland. "You were present at the affair of yesterday. You were of the party that were under the effects of intoxicating liquor, and made scandalous disturbance in coming through the towns?"— "I was present there, sir:"—"We cannot believe you had anything to do with the disgraceful occurrences on that occasion."—"You are quite right, sir, as to my not participating in them."—"Nothing can be learned from your comrades as to who the guilty parties are. It now becomes necessary for you to discover them."—"I have conscientious scruples against that, Sir."—"Your 'conscientious scruples' are a false sense of honor; the laws and the good order of the College require you to disclose these parties, or suffer the punishment due to their offence. You will be suspended from College at once."—"Mr. President, I can suffer for the offenses of others, but you cannot punish me for them. You can punish me for disobeying your orders, or the laws of the College. That punishment I accept."—"We should be very sorry to have to resort to that extremity."—"Yes, Sir, I very well know you would."—"Mr. President, I am willing to give account of myself at all times, to any that have the right to call me to account. But pardon me for saying that 1 think the requirement to give information against our comrades, though a practice in legal tribunals, is a false principle of College administration. It makes a boy an informer—a betrayer of confidence, which is much like a traitor. You speak, sir, of a false sense of honor. By false, you mean mistaken; and even if it were so, it is better to respect it than to try to break it down; for confidence between man and man is one of the lessons which the College should inculcate. I shall take patiently whatever consequences you may inflict. I know well my father will be proud to see me coming home for this; more so than I shall be to return here again." This was the bold little speech, just about *verbatim* as it was given on that really serious occasion. It was not in all respects sound, for the immunity contended for would conceal wrongdoing, and tend to perpetuate it. But it was at any rate a virtual protest against the sentence, and it evidently affected the good president's desire to continue the conversation. "Very well, Sir. You can go."

The boys were all gathered in the room, awaiting report. "I am going home, boys; there's no help for it."—"By Heaven, you shan't," cried the spokesman. "Boys let's go down and own up to cider, anyway. This shan't come on Jack." Their somewhat tardy frankness carried the case. All got a reprimand; and that was getting off too easy, after all.

HIS BOYHOOD STAMMER

∾

Perhaps the greatest challenge young Lawrence faced as a Bowdoin student was an affliction that had plagued him from childhood. No doubt the stuttering he describes below as a "positive disability" and "one of the miseries of life" created great anxiety that "affected habits and perhaps character" while it shaped his personality and personal interactions well into adulthood. It was important enough as a part of his life story that he devoted several paragraphs to its description and explanation.

∾

College tasks were very trying upon one tender point which the young man had long and painfully endeavored to keep a profound secret. One of the miseries of his life had been an impediment of speech which nothing but eternal vigilance kept from manifesting itself in horrible stammering. The initial letter "p," "b," and "l," well named in some of the grammars "close mutes," had well nigh made one of him. It was at times impossible to get off a word beginning with one of these letters unless it could be launched on a wave of breath, or when, forewarned, a run could be started for it which would carry it by sheer impetus—"pas de charge."* To be asked to start off—the first line of Virgil's *Bucolics,* "Tityre tu patulae recubans sub tegmine fagi"—made one envious of that rustic solitude, while to the expectant listener his refusal to plead brought astonishment and indignation, followed by the summary judgment fixed for him who obstinately stands mute.† Marvelous was the inventiveness developed in the endeavor to avoid these stumbling blocks, and the exploits in synonyms and circumlocutions were worthy of such praise as is lavished on classic authors for "copiousness of diction." But in truth, the sleepless anxiety on this score was a serious wear upon the nervous system. It was not much short of agonizing to contemplate an occasion where these close mutes were liable to be encountered. Intense observation and long habit in rapidly reconnoitering a written or printed page had given that military "coup d'oeil"—that quick and comprehensive eye—which is thought to be the peculiarity and prerogative of a born genius for command.‡

This positive disability added to a natural timidity of self-assertion, apt to disclose itself on untimely occasions in that stupidity called bashfulness, had a decided effect on habits both of speech and action, which placed one at a serious disadvantage. This also led to misunderstandings and unjust judgments. It was hard to submit to being thought stupid because in conversation the relevant answer or repartee was laid under embargo. It was humiliating to feel it necessary to avoid occasion and meetings where debate was likely to arise, and where to others, if he took part, it would really make no difference whether he knew what he was talking about or didn't know. It was a curious sensation to feel the nerves of shame and claws of wrath curling deep within when through dearth of synonym or poverty of the English language in mouth-opening words. it was necessary to pass by the plain befitting word in translation and offer a far-fetched phrase with what seemed ingenious and insulting stupidity, and then see the professor turn one gaze of impotent contempt for which there was also no synonym. and write down in his rank book one of the earliest of the Arabic numerals. It was the unkindest cut of all, however, when one desired to introduce mutual friends met on the street, or, still worse, in one's own room, and had to fight shy of it with futile arts and agonized expression,

---

* The French phrase *au pas de charge* means "at the double step."
† "Tityrus lying under the cover of a spreading beech tree."
‡ Literally translated, *coup d'oeil* means "stroke of the eye" and in English is replaced by "glance."

simply because their fathers had not had their names changed by order of court or "ticket of leave."

Such a condition was intolerable. It was not a thing to be avoided, but to be overcome. The methods of attack were simple, but they required resolution. This direct front attack would not be nearly so (asking and wearing as the eternal round of the anxious defensive). Two positive measures were determined on. The first required attention and will. The second demanded adroitness and tact, to move without drawing destructive observation. Operations commenced on the first line.

The thing now was to "do it." Not exactly in cart-wheel fashion, all at once. This wheel had to be taken by its spokes, one by one. This antagonist can only be beaten in detail. The trouble is that these close mutes shut you up. As long as you hold to them, you are dumb. The thing is to get away from them, as quick as possible. It must be a touch and go. Get a good breath behind it and turn on the will.

That is one way, and with care it is good nine times out of 10. The other way demands circumspection and consideration of others. Awkwardness brings detection and ridicule, which is failure. The principle here is to summon that power of the soul which expresses itself in the sense of rhythm. If you are coming to something which you can't speak, persuade yourself you are going to sing. Catch the pulse of time. Feel the emotion of it, and that will bear you on its motion. If the occasion is a great one, let your whole spirit be possessed with the trance, and give itself freely to the rhythmic sway and swing. You can do things now that were impossible before. It is not necessary to do this so badly and unskillfully as to draw the attention of your hearers from the things you are saying to the way you are saying them. That would very likely bring a laugh upon you and break you down. But you need not be ashamed. Anything that is worth saying, is worth singing. Let fools laugh if the wise learn. The old Spartans used to sing their laws for after-dinner pastime. And the Spartan laws were no laughing matter. Some space has been given to this subject because it was a serious one, an experience which affected habits and perhaps character, and the indirect effects of which may have reached into the whole of life. The writer of this knows that obstacles irremovable can be surmounted.

These first two years in College were on the whole a pretty severe experience. Hard study had to be done, not so much to keep up with the class as to get a good hold of fundamental studies and to acquire good habits of work. Fortunately the French had come easy, owing to the little saints militant at Ellsworth. That gave more time for other studies. But French under Professor Goodwin was something altogether now.* He did more than to "hear" lessons or even to teach. He broadened; he inspired; he integrated knowledge, and animated it; vitalized it. Studying French in this way, the boy began to see into Latin. He began to know something about language; more than that, he began to learn how to think into a thing, as well as to think it out.

He was not thinking specially of outward encouragements, but was as much gratified as surprised to find himself towards the close of the year appointed one of the assistant librarians under Professor Goodwin. This was understood as implying a high rank in the Department of Modern Languages, but had a greater value in that it betokened a certain good-will, or good opinion, on the part of that professor, and carried with it the privilege of personal and social relations with the professor and his family. To be frank, the appointment involved a little mortification on the part of the favored one; for he had been singularly and detrimentally neglectful of the privileges of the Library. One reason of this was that the regular College work did not leave much time for general reading, but the main reason was that a thirst or taste for reading had not been aroused. That was a department too much neglected in boyhood. The extreme notions prevailing in the household as to "novels" had not left much on the "free list" that was interesting. An entreaty for permission to read Cooper's *Deerslayer*, being denied perhaps through fear that the title had an ambiguous sound or misleading spelling in its first syllable, it resulted that, with the exception of a glance at a Sailor Song Book, certainly not much better reading offered him as a loan, which it may be said here was emphatically rejected, nothing like light reading had ever passed under his eyes, until the close of the sophomore year when by the appointment of the Professor of Rhetoric he wrote a "critique" on Hawthorne's *House of the Seven Gables*. That honored son of Bowdoin would have been amusingly amazed at the profoundness of the moral and literary judgments pronounced by the "debutante"!† Perhaps they had as much common sense as some emanating from professional sources.

The personal privileges connected with this appointment, together with the freedom of the hospitable household of Professor Alpheus S. J. Packard, whose son was a favorite classmate and most familiar friend,

---

* Daniel Raynes Goodwin (Bowdoin, class of 1832) was professor of modern languages (including French) from 1835 to 1853. He was also the college librarian from 1838 to 1853, when he left to become president of Trinity College.

† Nathaniel Hawthorne was a graduate of Bowdoin, class of 1825.

constituted the only social diversion from a strict College life indulged in for the first three years.*

Perhaps this remark should be qualified. For besides faithfully attending all the religious meetings, of his class Thursday evenings, of the "Circle" Saturday evenings, and the general College conference Sunday mornings, together with the required attendance on all church services, our much-saddled "Jack" undertook to carry on a Sunday-school held in a school-house two miles down the Bath road, walking there every Sunday afternoon through the burning summer months, for the College term then ran to the last of August, and never missing a service. It was, however, a delight to see that school-house overflowing with people, young and old, hearty in appreciation and abounding in homelike kindnesses. Forty years of stern and multi-form experience have hardened many qualities of body and spirit since those days, but the sight of that yellow schoolhouse to this hour starts a quiver in certain brain-cells we call heart-strings, with that curious craving for remembrance which wishes to know whether, in any lands, or worlds, there is so much as the trembling of a leaf to tell if one of those winged seeds blown off by summer winds found answering strength enough to live.†

But the summer and the task were over. The midway point of the College course was turned, and the good fortune was to be celebrated by a three-week vacation, in the midst of which should arrive also that other turning point and celebration, the twenty-first birthday, so called. But alas! for celebrations. The tension had been too great, the strain too unremitting. A fever had worked deep into the blood, which showed a strange pertinacity, and mockingly offset the "tension" by becoming itself intermittent and remittent; dogging the feeble footsteps of the patient from cover to cover, and holding him at bay, with a fight for life, for nine months. This was hard to bear, beyond the disability and pain. Was it perhaps a rebuke to the misjudged effort to gain a year by doubling tasks? At any rate there was nothing for it now but to "fall back" a year, that is to stand still and let the class go on. The momentous birthday had but a mournful celebration. It was relieved by a touch of the comical in the pertinacity with which the half delirious brain of the patient battled the common saying that this was his twenty-first birthday. Manifestly it was his twenty-second. He had

---

* Alpheus Spring Packard (Bowdoin, class of 1816) was professor of ancient languages and classical literature from 1824 to 1865. His son, William Alfred Packard (Bowdoin, class of 1851), became a professor at Dartmouth and Princeton.

† The schoolhouse to which he refers is in the vicinity of what is now the Cooks Corner shopping area.

completed his twenty-first year on the day before, and was now upon his twenty-second birthday, one day on towards his twenty-second year. That was only a "lucid interval" of argument; but the conclusion was one of fact. In the crisis of this long struggle the attending physician had given up. Whereupon the long-enduring mother thought herself justified in discharging him from further service. This was a hard thing to do, because he was not only deacon of the church, but the salaried family physician, and most intimate friend, exercising as much freedom of the house as any member of the family.

Moreover a Homeopathic physician was to be called in his stead. This theory was open to ridicule; but the practical results were beyond cavil. By some mysterious metempsychosis another spirit seemed to be put into that body which called it back to life and harmony and health. From that time the hygienic system of this school was put into practice in that family and the good old friend and deacon had not much more to do professionally but draw his salary, which he regularly did.

But the patient learned patience. The cloud that overhung was "big with mercies," and it "broke in blessings." The loving care of mother and sister was a communion and a sacrament. And in convalescence the interchange of salient rejoinder and surrejoinder woke in that hushed house the slumbering spirits of the old Huguenot hilarity.

Falling back a year was not so pleasant. To go into a class below was the reverse of College honors. And one would more than miss his old classmates, when he had to see them every day and be not of them. But it must be this or give up College. So in that short summer of freshening health, it was only amusement to review familiar studies, while for once a real vacation was enjoyed at home, among the fields and woods, and birds and beasts, held all so dear.

Returning to College for his junior year, the exile's class were Seniors! But the lower class knew him well, as he had never worn a mask before them in the "hazy" days of yore. Indeed he enjoyed the rare felicity of confidential membership of two classes at once, thinking how happy Jacob must have been in loyally holding on to Leah and lovingly taking in Rachel. Junior year was devoted to good solid work. That was regarded the strong year in College. It is not so clear now what made it so. The mathematics had a stiff course, and gave wholesome work to those who meant to master it. Beginning German was elementary work. But absolutely successful in every one of those easy lessons, it is really surprising what mastery one will have achieved at the year's end. Then there was time for taking up under the same broadening guidance the simple sonorous Spanish.

One passage from the very first reading lesson showing the remarkable quality of sonorousness in the Spanish language even in the plainest prose, the rush of forty years and the roar of forty battles have not banished from the brain. "Todo in esta territorio classico respire historia; todo requerda los tiempos de la cavalliera, y los glorias pasadas de la Antigua Espagna."

"Todo en este territorio classico respire historia; todo requerda los tiempos de la cavalleria, y los glorias pasadas de la Antigua Espana."*

The far off goal of Latin was lamely plodded after. There was cold strength in Juvenal, and warm strength in the *Agricola* of Tacitus; something for the backbone, and something for the heart.† Then a new great orb had risen on the eastern horizon in the person of Professor Calvin E. Stowe, with his Hebrew literature, and his genius of a wife;—surely a double-star, this!‡ Our whilom corn-stalk initiate of the bass-viol got to fingering the Chapel organ, and being shortly afterwards organist of the Lockwood Musical Society, which had charge of the Chapel music, he was sent by the president of the College to Boston to study the best methods of conducting the "antiphonal chants" for the Sunday services then held for the first time in the beautiful new Chapel, which proved too purely "Romanesque" for services in Puritanical style, and these antiphonal chants were frowned upon by some influential people as savoring too much of the "Romanesque" for a good orthodox College.

The Professor of Rhetoric had touched a slumbering chord by endorsing on the margin of a College "theme" the remark: "If the writer of this will hold his imaginative powers well in hand, he will be heard from in due time." It was not perfectly clear how this should be taken. The "writer" was not aware that he had a habit of letting his fancy run away with his facts; but looking into the facts of this case faithfully he discovered that the quick perception of analogies, and the instinctive action of the "law" of the association of ideas had led, perhaps, to a tendency to overload a subject with illustration.

So the admonition was taken sensitively and seriously, that is to say, sensibly, and that friendly rebuke which should be best encouragement, and indicating that attention should be given on to "composition," the symmetrical and organ arrangement of material. Consequently, the student

---

* "Everything in this country breathes classic history. All remember the days of Cavalleria, and the glories of ancient Spain."

† Publius Cornelius Tacitus was a Roman senator and historian whose works included a biography of his father-in-law, Agricola, conqueror of Britain. Juvenal, or Decimus Iunius Iuvenalis, was a Roman poet who wrote the *Satires*.

‡ Calvin E. Stowe was professor of natural and revealed religion from 1850 to 1852.

now betook himself to rigorous study of Whateley's *Rhetoric,** and practice in argumentative composition. It was a little strange that notwithstanding his mental and physical disabilities and inaptitudes, before referred to, he found himself awarded at the end of this year the College prizes both in composition and in oratory. It is quite likely that if it were not for these disabilities so manifestly to be overcome, these prizes would not have been taken.

A "Junior Part" in the Public Exhibition at the close of the year indicating good rank in general scholarship was another recognition of honest work. The performer at this exhibition took a notion to show how in certain poetic conceptions the "spluttering" German language could express not only deep tones of feeling but sonorous utterances equally with English. He gave a translation from Ossian's *Fingal,* one line of which still lingers in the ear.

"Der Geist des Loda schrie, als zusammen gerollt er steig auf den Schwingen des Windes hinauf."†

But, "Of all good things there are three," says the German proverb, and so were finished three College years.

Senior year should have confined the student still more closely to his proper work. But various influences distracted his attention, to the detriment, perhaps, of strict College rank, but whether on the whole, to his injury it is not so easy to determine. For one thing, he became "conductor" of the Church choir in the beautiful Gothic Church of the "First Parish" which held its original territorial organization, and was in official relations with the College. This choir gained such proficiency that it was invited to give public concerts in neighboring towns. It came about also that in the last half of the year, the conductor became organist as well.

Another attraction was "The Round Table," a literary circle meeting every fortnight for the reading and discussion of original papers. These were prepared with great care, for the membership was of a high order, and a critical and exacting spirit.

It is fair to say that several of those young men and women have been "heard from" since, in honorable paths of literature. But chief of privileges were the "Saturday Evenings" at Mrs. Stowe's.‡ On these occasions a chosen circle of friends, mostly young, were favored with the freedom of her

---

* *Elements of Rhetoric,* by English rhetorician Richard Whately, was published in 1828.

† "The spirit of Loda shrieked, as he rolled up to join the wings of the wind." From "Fingal," a poem by eighteenth-century Scottish poet James Macpherson, which he claimed to have based on early Gaelic legends. The Spirit of Loda is said to be symbolic of the Scandinavian god Odin.

‡ Harriet Beecher Stowe's husband, Calvin, mentioned above, was professor of natural and revealed religion at Bowdoin.

house, the rallying point being, however, the reading before publication, of the successive chapters of her *Uncle Tom's Cabin*, and the frank discussion of them.* It was manifest that the author was least of all impressed with their merit, and surely no one there dreamed of the fame that was to follow. The sweetness of her spirit, and her genuine interest for others, and her charming hospitalities, even when the preparations for them fell mostly upon her own hands, were what drew to her the hearts of all. All these outside attractions—if they can be so misnamed—led to many social and personal engagements, one of which was in the highest degree intensified after graduation.

It would not do to be out late nights whatever else befall, for the dubious distinction of being selected by Professor Cleaveland as his special assistant in Chemistry and Physics required one to be up at five o'clock in the morning to see that all the powers of the elements were duly disposed for the six o'clock lecture.† As this included Professor's good temper, the service was a somewhat anxious one. The chief dread was however that of taking a final "honor" in his department, which was likely to result, as it did in this case, in having an unforeseen problem given in Astronomy, at the grand public examination, which took the shape this time of being called to cover one side of the mathematical room with the detailed demonstration of an eclipse of the sun to take place in a year which modern students of prophecy have determined to be some time after the "end of the world."

An entertainment "extra" in every sense of the word, was the study of Italian, and the reading of Dante and Tasso under the guidance and inspiration of Professor Goodwin. In another direction, Professor Upham's three volumes on The Intellect, The Sensibilities and The Will gave opportunity for practical illustrations in all these powers of the mind.‡ Decidedly the highest intellectual exercises were those held with the President on the great argument of "Butler's Analogy."§ Whatever may be said about the present utility of an argument on this ground, or of this as running the risk of the fallacy of "proving too much," it is certain that a mind that followed the President with any faithfulness could not but gain most useful discipline under that consummate master and suave spirit whose subtle dialectic was

---

* Stowe is said to have written her epic novel in the parlor of the Stowe home on Federal Street and in her husband's office in Appleton Hall when the house became too noisy and distracting. Published in 1852, the book sold more copies in the nineteenth century than any other book except the Bible.

† Parker Cleaveland taught mathematics at Bowdoin for twenty years, and chemistry, minerology, and natural literature for fifty-three years.

‡ Thomas C. Upham was professor of mental and moral philosophy from 1824 to 1867.

§ Bishop Joseph Butler wrote his infamous *Analogy of Religion, Natural and Revealed, to the Constitution and Course of Nature* in 1736.

like the exquisite edge of Saladin's cimetar one airy sweep of which would
in the flash of an eye cut asunder the finest veil ever woven of women or
worn of man.

GRADUATION FROM BOWDOIN

~

*By sitting back a year due to his illness, Chamberlain graduated with the class of
1852. This was important because the commencement exercises of that year included
the celebration of the fiftieth anniversary of the college. Accomplished Bowdoin gradu-
ates such as Nathaniel Hawthorne, Henry Wadsworth Longfellow, and Franklin
Pierce, who had only recently become the Democratic nominee for U.S. president,
returned to Brunswick for the occasion. Reports said that 3,000 people sought out a
place for the ceremonies held inside the First Parish Church adjacent to the campus.
Chamberlain spoke from the high Gothic pulpit as the fourth speaker in the program. In the presence of these illustrious guests, as well as his family, his childhood
stammer returned.***

~

All these late laxities did not prevent our senior from receiving a Commencement assignment of the first rank. He thought it would be a sympathetic and fining subject for this occasion to present himself on the arena
with *The Last Gladiatorial Show at Rome.*

All would perhaps have gone well had it not been for the abnormal
action of that mysterious "tertium quid" called "the nervous system."† But
the presence in the close-crowding and crowded galleries of certain friends
whose love and pride were at utmost tension, gave occasion for the evil
one to interpose some of his mockeries of human ambition. Some slight
occurrence among the distinguished audience, for that was the occasion of
the 50th anniversary of the organization of the College, and all the digni-
taries of the nation were represented there, disturbed the anxious balance
of the speaker's self-possession, and he stopped short. Our gladiator was

---

* An original program from the commencement exercises is held in the Chamberlain Family Papers in the Special Collections Department of Fogler Library at the University of Maine at
Orono.

† Literally translated as "the third thing," the term *tertium quid* refers to an unknown element in
company with two that are known.

hit; the adversary had broken down his guard. For a moment all around him swum and swayed into a mist. But he only reeled, half-turned, and paced the stage, grasping some evidently extemporaneous and strangely far-fetched phrases, then suddenly whirling to the front, with more blood in his face than would have flowed from Caesar's "morituri salutamus," he delivered his conclusion straight out from the shoulder like those who are determined to die early.* That public failure lessened the pang of parting. The crestfallen champion was glad to get out of town.

This experience revived the question whether it was best to go to West Point where he would have to stand his hand, or to the Theological Seminary where he could read his sermons. Was not this "a call to preach"? At any rate the latter was nearer home, and the base of supplies. So that fall saw the gladiator in the Bangor Theological Seminary. But he could at least support himself. By organizing classes in German in the city, and by being appointed supervisor of schools in his native town as well as "playing the organ" in the church across the river, he earned an ample support, and enjoyed the varied field of operations. Being lame in Latin and fresh in German, he resolved to lead all his "Theology" in these two languages. This presented vital questions in widely variant lights. But the professor held him pretty stiffly to the "old school," though the main current of the sentiment of his class trended quite the other way. Perhaps it was owing to the inward Conflicts growing out of this, that when appointed in the middle of the course one of the speakers at the exhibition of the Rhetorical Society, he took for subject "The Melancholy of Genius," in which lugubrious effort he managed not to break down. The Hebrew language had great fascination for him, with its strong, old, three letter verbal roots, its virile forces, its susceptibility to sense-impressions, and its primeval conception of time, or rather, tense, the perfect and the imperfect; the past and the future; these two embracing all the conceptions of action; for the past resolved upon he comes the future, and the present but a flash, for while you speak it the future becomes the past.

But thinking now of the mission fields of the Orient, strenuous attention was turned to Arabic and Syriac, the reflex effect of which woke new concepts of thought, new images of life.

In the senior year the student wrote the four required sermons for criticism and was sent out to preach them as a "supply" on several occasions, resulting in receiving four different invitations to important policies

---

* Literally translated as "We who are about to die salute you," "Morituri Te Salutamus" was the title of a Longfellow poem written for the fiftieth anniversary of the Bowdoin class of 1824.

before his graduation. But close upon the end, while preparing his graduating part for the public exercises, he received notice of his appointment to deliver the "Master's Oration," representing his class for the second degree at Bowdoin College. There was not time to prepare two different orations, and the College accepted a repetition of what he should give at the Seminary the week before. It was perhaps a perfunctory thing for them; but not so for him. The conjuncture demanded his best. And so far as the time permitted, he gave it.

When he stepped upon that College stage, the flush on his face was far different from that with which he had left it three years before. He had taken for his subject "Law and Liberty." The main argument of this was that the superabounding life lavished in the universe was proof that the play of infinite freedom was to work out the will of infinite law. The whole universe showed that freedom was a part of law.

The effect of this among those who heard it was an utter and overwhelming surprise to its author. The newspaper notices made him feel as if he had wakened in another world. Dr. Joseph P. Thompson wrote to the New York "Independent" a notice that opened a new current of thought in the mind of the young master of arts.[*] Life had another horizon. There might be a duty of choice as well as the power of it. There might be for him an illustration of his own doctrine of the freedom which subserves highest law.

The College the very next day offered him some of the work Professor Stowe had just left, and he took his place at the opening of the next term as special instructor in Logic and Natural Theology, with the charge of the Freshman Greek. His brother Horace was now entering his junior year. And John, the next brother, entered freshman, at this Commencement of 1855. So the three brothers were together on different grades as they had been at the foremast of the "man of war."

MARRIAGE AND CAREER

~

Having completed his education and accepted a permanent position on the Bowdoin faculty, Chamberlain felt he was ready to start a family. In December 1855, after

---

[*] Joseph P. Thompson was pastor of the Broadway Tabernacle Church in New York and a leading Congregationalist. Chamberlain's Bowdoin classmate Oliver Otis Howard was a layman in the church. Along with Leonard Bacon, Richard Storrs, and Henry Bowen, Thompson founded the newspaper *Independent* in 1848, primarily to combat the extension of slavery.

a four-year courtship, he married Frances Caroline Adams. "Fannie," as she was
known to family and friends, had grown up as the adopted daughter of Rev. George
Adams, pastor of the First Parish Church adjacent to the Bowdoin campus. The two
had met while Chamberlain led the church choir and Fannie played the organ. Soon
after marrying, they bought a small home across Maine Street from both the church
and the Bowdoin campus. Less than a year later, Fannie gave birth to the first of
five children, only two of whom would live beyond their first year.

~

As the three angles of a triangle are equal to two right angles, and as two
right angles are easily resolvable into a straight line, it seemed good for
the young man to lay out his life course and establish a new family headquarters. Accordingly in December of that year he married Miss Frances
C. Adams, a native of Boston, on the father's side descended from a col-
lateral branch of the Massachusetts Adamses, and on the mother's from the
Wyllyses and Dyers of Connecticut, early governors and secretaries of that
colony, and hence direct descendent of "Mabel Harlakenden."*

At the next Commencement he was elected Professor of Rhetoric and
Oratory. The very irony of fate for one who had so struggled against what
he had supposed disqualifying disabilities in this department.

In the golden days of the Indian summer of that year, there came to
his house an angel of God, who left his living smile for the loving earth part
of the infinite heaven! There was a daughter of the house.† Now a new life
was begun indeed for all in that house. There were more things between
the heaven and the earth than were dreamed of in our philosophy. There
were revelations that startled the pupil parents.

They had taken the little one to church one day when she was two
years old, and after service all remained for the "Communion." The sacred
elements being distributed, she as of course was passed by. She nestled up
to her mother and asked what this all meant. She was told that they were
remembering God. "Why then do they leave me out? Don't they know
that I came from God a great deal littler while ago and I can remember him
a great deal better than any of these big people can? They forget me, but he
does not." And she was so grieved it was thought best to take her home,
where we with her, Remembered God. That Indian summer there came

---

* Mabel Harlakenden married Colonel John Haynes who became governor of the Colony of
Connecticut in 1639.

† Grace Dupee Chamberlain, whom her parents called "Daisy," was born October 16, 1856.

from the same remembering heaven a son, "drawing from out the vast and striking his being into bounds."*

At the Commencement of 1857 the young professor, in addition to his other duties, was placed in charge of the instruction in the German language and literature, as well as of the optional instruction in the Spanish language. Some assistance being provided in his own department, he also in the second year formed an optional class in the Old Norse language and commenced a systematic course of lectures on the Anglo-Saxon and Early English language and literature.

In 1861 he was elected Professor of Modern Languages, and entered at once upon the duties of that important department. The five years work in the College thus far would have been a severe tax upon ordinary strength, but the vigorous tone was kept up by putting every available hour of free-dom into outdoor exercise. Many a good outing was taken with congenial spirit, among the students, either among the trout-brooks, or along the shore of the bay, and sometimes on the bay itself. Some more than ordinary college friendships were thus formed which have not grown cold through all the following years.

Then, too, the hard-working professor had been able to purchase and half pay for the modest cottage where many a young professor had started out before him. Henry W. Longfellow being the first, who took his bride here for their beginning in life. This had ample ground for as much garden as one man could well manage, and here he might be seen if anybody was up early enough, at five o'clock in the morning, digging and scratching away at the genial and much-loved earth. One good consequence of these early exercises entirely unforeseen, was that a hard-headed old sea captain, now president of the principal bank of the village, in his early drives for good health and habits got an occasional sight of our gardener, and liking these industrious habits, came forward without solicitation, and offered him all the money he wanted to pay for his house or anything else on his own personal note, and his own time. This kindness was accepted.†

But in the meantime had come a great grief and loss in the death of the nearest brother, whose brilliant gifts and accomplishments as a coun-selor and jury lawyer gave promise of a remarkable career. The friendship and sympathy between the brothers were of no common order, and the bereavement was a deep one.‡

---

* Their second child, Harold Wyllys Chamberlain, was born October 10, 1858.

† This was Captain Joseph Badger, president of the Pejepscot Bank in Brunswick.

‡ Horace Beriah Chamberlain, whom the family called "Hod," the second of four Chamberlain brothers, died in December 1861.

Then, too, a second daughter had come to that house, who left but a summer smile and aching hearts, as she departed with the flowers.*

But even mightier things than personal griefs then took possession of every heart. The flag of the nation had been insulted. The honor and authority of the Union had been defied. The integrity and the existence of the people of the United States had been assailed in open and bitter war. The North was at last awake to the intent and the magnitude of the Rebellion. The country was roused to the peril and duty of the hour.†

~

Well into the summer of 1862, the Civil War was not going well for President Lincoln. A four-month long campaign against the Confederate capitol at Richmond had bogged down into what now seemed an inevitable and embarrassing failure. Thousands of American lives had been lost without bringing the war any closer to a conclusion. Hopeful that by reinforcing the army in Virginia he could salvage the effort, the president needed to ask the states for more troops.

Coming on the heels of growing military disasters in the South, however, and with midterm elections lurking just five months away, he could not ask the country to offer up more of its sons, fathers, husbands, and neighbors.

"I would publicly appeal to the country for this new force," he wrote to Secretary of State William H. Seward, "were it not that I fear a general panic and stampede would follow."

Instead, either he or Seward, or both, devised a plan to meet with several Northern governors in New York and draft a letter from them in which they would "respectfully request" that Lincoln ask them for more troops, "if it meets with your entire approval." They backdated the letter a few days to June 28, 1862, so it would appear to have been initiated prior to the latest military disaster in Virginia.

Maine's Governor Israel Washburn, a founder of the still-young Republican Party and a childhood neighbor and friend of Lincoln's vice president, Hannibal Hamlin, was the first name among the eighteen signatories at the bottom of this letter that provided political cover for Lincoln to issue a call to the states for 300,000 more troops. By joining his fellow governors in the call for additional soldiers, Washburn was committing his state to recruiting, training, and equipping a total of 4,000 more Mainers into four new regiments of infantry, each with a handful of sought-after military appointments for the governor to dole out whether the reasons for these

* The Chamberlain's fourth child, Emily Stelle Chamberlain, was their second child who died within a year of birth.
† It is interesting to note that, decades after its conclusion, Chamberlain described several major themes of the war but made not even the slightest mention of slavery.

choices were military, political, or both. When Maine's quota of 4,000 new soldiers had been enlisted, there were an additional 1,000 enlistees awaiting assignment to a regiment. So, Governor Washburn ordered the formation of one more infantry regiment, numerically, the state's twentieth.

～

The summons rang almost strangely in the ears of one who once rejected West Point because it led to "being a soldier in time of peace." An irresistible impulse stirred him to have a hand in this business now that the moral forces of the people had summoned the physical to their defense. So on being chosen professor for life in this chair of modern languages, with the special privilege of a leave of absence for two years to visit Europe and perfect himself in these tongues, he telegraphed the governor of the state: "I have leave of absence for two years to visit Europe, but I wish to know whether I have a country. Can you make any use for me?" The reply was, "Come and see me. I am organizing a regiment." This interview showed that the governor's thought went far beyond the young professor's dream. He was thinking only of some staff position where the immediate responsibility would not be heavy, and he could have opportunity to learn practical military duties. Nobody now looked upon the war as sport, or a short madness; it was serious business. The Army of the Potomac, after terrible experiences, was abandoning its base of operations, and was assembling before Washington for a new and desperate campaign. There was a new call for troops, and the pressure was great. The new troops must be thrown into the midst of the bitter and tremendous struggle. It was not wise, to say the least, to take the responsibility of an important command with such certain prospects, without experience. This was the young man's response to the Governor. "Give the colonelcy of the regiment to some regular officer now in the field. I will take a subordinate position, and learn and earn my way to the command."

With wise or unwise forethought the Professor had not consulted his colleagues about this movement. But the matter came out through the papers. Then there was a strife at home over this case which was a good rehearsal for the future field. The "faculty" objected. They remonstrated with the governor assuring him that the young professor had no military stuff in him. They even sent a representative to the capital to demonstrate that he was no fighter, but only a mild-mannered commonplace student.

～

The representative who conveyed the message was Maine's attorney general, Josiah Drummond, who informed the governor by letter that "His old classmates etc. here say, you have been deceived: that C. is nothing at all: that is the universal expression of those who know him."

It was indeed a strange exhibition of affection. But this was not the ruling motive. The professors were men of military experience in the religious contests for the control of the College. They had learned grand tactics. The young professor held for them a strategic position. This chair was much sought for; and those competent to fill it were for the most part, not of the strict orthodox persuasion. In case this chair should become vacant, as the experiences and prospects of war rendered highly probable, the chances were that it would be filled by one of the adverse party.

But they reckoned without both their hosts. The young colleague was not coward enough to let go his purpose under such injurious misrepresentations, and the governor well knew the father and grandfather of his candidate and had no thought of letting his own judgment be superseded. The result was that in two weeks from the granting of the leave of absence to go to Europe, the professor was in camp at Portland organizing the 20th Regiment of Infantry as lieutenant colonel.

The parting demonstrations at Brunswick were not pathetic. The faculty offered no congratulations. The village Newspaper announced that Professor Chamberlain and Nichols, the tailor, had entered the service, and both deserved great credit.* This was the judicial equipoise of the editorial mind, and helped to smooth things over. The kindly and generous citizens of Brunswick and Topsham presented to the young officer the most splendid and famous horse in the region, with a full set of elegant equipments.† In his own little home, there were earnest faces and loyal and stout hearts. Like so many others beginning life, they gave their all in the hour of supreme peril of their Country.

---

* James H. Nichols helped raise a company of men and was appointed a lieutenant in Company K of the 20th Maine. His habit of "drinking intoxicating liquor to excess," however, prevented his further promotion.

† The horse, a dapple gray known locally as "the Staples horse," was said to be worth the enormous sum of $900, about the value of a modest rural home at that time. Chamberlain named him "Prince," and his handsome appearance attracted much attention during his service in the army, including that of President Abraham Lincoln. It was for this same reason, however, that Chamberlain avoided riding him when in close proximity to the enemy.

∾

Here, just as Chamberlain began his military career, the typescript ends. The reason for this appears to be that the old warrior had by then written many pieces about his wartime experiences and adding another was of no real value to posterity.

To fill out this important aspect of his life and career, the following chapters, written mostly by his own hand, help tell the story of the three most significant battles in which he was engaged. These are Fredericksburg in December 1862, Gettysburg in July 1863, and Petersburg in June 1864—and finally, the surrender of Robert E. Lee's army at Appomattox Court House in Virginia in April 1865.

∾

2

MY STORY OF FREDERICKSBURG

❧

Following the regiment's formation just outside Portland in August 1862, it was mustered into service and sent by train to Boston and then by steamship to Washington, D.C. After a few days being provided with rifled muskets at the U.S. arsenal there, news of the invasion of Maryland by General Lee's Army of Northern Virginia created a heightened emergency. In response, various units then in Washington, including the 20th Maine, were ordered to march seventy miles northwest to join other unions forces already in the region. For the men of the newly formed regiment, untrained and physically unprepared for a forced march, the experience was painful.

The harsh necessity of the hurried march did nothing to endear the footsore men to their new commander, Colonel Adelbert Ames of Rockland. Ames had been raised on board his father's sailing ships where discipline—often harsh—was a top priority. His three years as a West Point cadet had done nothing to soften that edge, nor had his service in an artillery battery at Bull Run when, severely wounded, he refused to be taken from the field until the loss of blood caused his collapse. Years later, he would be awarded a Medal of Honor for that experience, but just now he faced the daunting task of leading a group of untrained, undisciplined volunteers into battle.

The 20th Maine was, mercifully, held out of the fighting at Antietam on September 17, just two weeks after they had departed their home state, and they spent the next two months training under the relentless, unforgiving eye of Colonel Ames. In late November, the army began to move southward with designs on threatening and eventually capturing the Confederate capitol at Richmond.

This article appeared in the January 1913 issue of Cosmopolitan, *a magazine owned and run by William Randolph Hearst. The issue commemorated the fiftieth anniversary of the Battle of Fredericksburg, and Chamberlain was paid the handsome sum of $500 to write it.*

Fredericksburg, Virginia, is a city on the banks of the Rappahannock River about sixty miles south of Washington, D.C. In 1862 it was home to about 5,000 inhabitants and had struggled to find a prosperous commercial identity since the rail line between Washington and Richmond had bypassed it, considerably weakening the importance of the city's canal and port. By the time the army's commander General Ambrose Burnside sent his first troops across the river to attack well-established Confederate lines just to the west, most of the inhabitants had fled. Eleven weeks after President Lincoln issued his Emancipation Proclamation, and less than three weeks before it took effect legally, as many as 10,000 slaves in the region fled toward Union lines. No Civil War–era military attack was more obvious nor the enemy more forewarned than in the days leading up to Burnside's ill-fated frontal assault on Lee's entrenched army that began on December 11, 1862.

~

December of 1862 found the Army of the Potomac not in the best of cheer. After the hardfought battle of Antietam, McClellan thought chiefly to recruit his army, and moved but slowly to follow the discomfited Lee. Before we had left that field, President Lincoln came to look over the pitiable scene and the heroic men who had made it, its dead, and themselves immortal. Being a guest at our Fifth Corps headquarters, we had the opportunity to discern something more of that great spirit than was ordinarily revealed in those rugged features and deep, sad eyes. The men conceived a sympathy and an affection for him that was wonderful in its intensity.

To cheer him and them, a grand review of the battered army was given. Lincoln was a good horseman, and this showed him to new advantage. He took in everything with earnest eyes. As the reviewing cavalcade passed along our lines, where mounted officers were stationed in front of their commands, he checked his mount to draw McClellan's attention to my horse, whose white-dappled color and proud bearing made me almost too conspicuous on some occasions.*

Impatience at McClellan's slowness and irresolution, or some other influence at Washington, prompted the removal of this commander and the substitution of Burnside; and, as somehow a sequence of this, the removal of Fitz John Porter from command of the Fifth Corps and the appointment of Hooker to the place. Whatever justification there was for these changes,

---

* When they learned of Chamberlain's decision to join the army, local supporters presented him with an extraordinary gift, a dapple-gray horse said to be worth the enormous sum of nearly $1000. As Chamberlain implies, it made him "almost too conspicuous" a target on a battlefield, so he often switched with some other rearward officer so as to present a less attractive target to the enemy.

the sundering of long-familiar ties brought a strain on the heart-strings of many men, but it must be remarked in their honor that no murmuring or lack of loyal and cheerful obedience ever betrayed their sorrow. Things were not brightened when Burnside, in taking command, modestly but unwisely intimated his unfitness for it. There was a tendency to take him at his word—especially among the high-ranking generals—and the men could not help knowing it.

For another change, the army was reorganized in three grand divisions: the right, consisting of the Second and Ninth corps, commanded by Sumner; the center, the Third and Fifth corps, commanded by Hooker; and the left, the First and Sixth Corp, commanded by Franklin.

We were soon aware of a decided division of opinion about the best plan for the prosecution of the campaign. Burnside proposed to give up the pursuit of Lee's army then gathered mainly in the vicinity of Culpeper and to strike for Petersburg and Richmond. Halleck, General-in-Chief, did not approve of this as it exposed Washington to a backstroke from Lee. Nor did the President. Burnside then offered a compromise plan: to cross the fords of the Rappahannock above Fredericksburg and seize the heights around that city, making his line of supplies the railroad between Fredericksburg and Acquia Creek on the Potomac. Halleck still disapproved, and the President only reluctantly assented. But to the astonishment of both, Burnside, instead of crossing at the upper ford, moved down the north bank of the river and took position directly confronting Fredericksburg.

LEE PREPARES A DEATH TRAP

Burnside's intention was now manifest—to cross the Rappahannock at this front. This would require the service of pontoons and the demand for them went promptly to Washington. This, of course, displeased the authorities there, a direct assault on Fredericksburg being no part of the plan approved; and there was a long wait for pontoons. In turn, this gave Lee time to confront our purpose with his usual promptitude and skill. He seemed to have had perfect knowledge of Burnside's movements and plans. He lost no time in seizing the crests and wooded slopes which surround Fredericksburg, where he strongly posted his infantry covered by breastworks and rifle pits. The ground afforded every advantage for his artillery, both for cover and efficiency, and enabled him to dispose his whole line so as to bring a front and flank fire upon any possible assault of ours. His chief of artillery said to scrutinizing Longstreet: "Our guns are so placed that we can rake the whole field as with a fine-tooth comb. A chicken could not live on that field." Other batteries were so directed as to sweep every pontoon bridge we could lay at the base of the principal crest behind the city some of Lee's best troops manned a breast-high stone wall, before which after history lays direful memories.

At last, on the 25th of November, the pontoons began to arrive. It requires skill and level heads to lay a pontoon bridge. But our brave engineers found their skill baffled and the level of their heads much disturbed by the hot fire from the well-manned rifle-pits on the opposite shore, and from the sharpshooters in the houses above them, and had to give up the task. Then our nearest batteries opened a terrific fire on those offensive shelters and their occupants, under which some of the houses were set afire, the smoke and flame giving a wild background to the tense and stirring scene. In the tumult and shadow of this some daring men of the 7th Michigan and the 19th Massachusetts forged to the front, manned the forsaken boats, and pushed across, clearing all before them. Howard's division soon crossed over and seized and held that portion of the town.

I may present an incident of this bombardment which impressed me at the time, and has stood vividly in memory ever since I was near one of our upper batteries—I think Benjamin's, of the 2d Regular—observing the effect of the fire, when a staff officer of Sumner's rode up and, pointing across, bent low in his saddle and said with softened voice, "Captain, do you see that white shaft over yonder in the green field above those houses?" "I do, sir," was the reply. "That is the tomb of Washington's mother," rejoined the staff-officer. "Let your guns spare that!" "They will, sir!" was the answer, as if the guns themselves knew. I turned away, thoughtful of many things.

Next morning the bridges were laid without opposition; Lee doubtless thought his guns would do better work when crowds of men were crossing. Two bridges were in front of our right, Sumner's ground; one for us, in Hooker's front, just opposite the lower city—one being thought enough, as we were not expected to make our principal crossing there; two a mile or more below, in Franklin's front. Lee's dispositions for an offensive-defensive battle were such that it became necessary for us to cover his entire front with artillery for possible chances; so 149 guns were put in position on the north bank of the Rappahannock.

BURNSIDE'S PLAN OF BATTLE

The plan of battle was now made known to us. Sumner was to make an attack and secure a lodgment in the upper and central portion of the town; Franklin was to make the main assault a mile or two below, turn Lee's right, and take his main position in flank. To support Franklin in this, two divisions of our Third Corps were sent him, thus giving him sixty thousand effective men. Hooker, with the rest of our grand division, was to move up to the north bank, near the middle pontoon bridge, ready to cross there or to go to the support of either right or left as should be needed.*

So we were held in reserve. It may be thought that we were glad to be kept out of the fight, at least for the present. But I take occasion to say that in forming for a great fight it is not regarded as a very special favor to be "held in reserve." The "holding" is most likely, not for long; and it holds in itself peculiar stress and strain. Waiting and watching, intent and anxious, stirred by the pulse of manhood and the contagion of comradeship, conscious of strength to help, but forbidden to strike, all this wears sorely on every generous spirit. And that other not unmanly impulse—if the worst is coming, let us meet it—may have its part, too, in the drama. It is really less trying to go in first and deliver your blow in the flush of spirit and strength, with the feeling that if the worst comes, you will be reenforced or "relieved," than to be held back till some dire disaster calls, when the life-and-death grapple clinches, and you must recover the lost ground or die trying. Or, on the other hand, to be called to advance in triumph over a field already carried— something then is lacking to the manly sense of service rendered according to strength.

THE DEATH-DELIVERING STONE WALL

Our division, Griffin's, of the Fifth Corps, was massed near the Lacy house, opposite the city. We could plainly see the fierce struggle of our Second and Ninth Corps to surmount those flaming crests behind the city. Lines first steadily moving forward in perfect order and array, the flag high poised and leading; checked and broken somewhat on each successive rise under the first range of shot and shell; no musket replying—for this would have

---

* The numerical advantage in troops overall heavily favored the Union forces. At roughly 120,000 soldiers to the Confederacy's 78,000, Burnside had more than one and a half times the force available to him. Burnside also had a huge advantage in food, supplies, and ammunition, given the presence of the Potomac River just fifteen miles to the east.

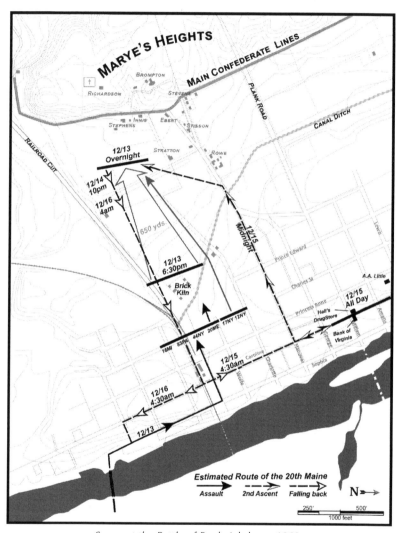

MARYE'S HEIGHTS

MAIN CONFEDERATE LINES

BROMPTON

RICHARDSON

STEVENS

PLANK ROAD

CANAL DITCH

INNIS

EBERT

STEPHENS

STISSON

RAILROAD CUT

STRATTON

ROWE

12/13
Overnight

12/14
10pm

650 yds.

12/16
4am

12/15
Midnight

Prince Edward

12/13
6:30pm

Brick
Kiln

Charles St

A.A. Little

12/15
All Day

16MI 83PA 44NY 20ME 17NY 12NY

Princess Anne

Hall's
DrugStore

Bank of
Virginia

12/15
4:30am

Caroline

Sophia

12/16
4:30am

12/13

Estimated Route of the 20th Maine

Assault   2nd Ascent   Falling back

N

250'   500'

1000 feet

Scene at the Battle of Fredericksburg, 1862.

been worse than useless— but bright bayonets fixed, ready at the final reach to sweep like a sharp wave-crest over the enemy's rock-like barrier. Right on! Then, reaching the last slope before and beneath the death-delivering stone wall, suddenly illumined by a sheet of flame, and in an instant the whole line sinking as if swallowed up in earth, the bright flags quenched in gloom, and only a writhing mass marking that high-tide halt of uttermost manhood and supreme endeavor. Then a slow back-flowing, with despairing effort here and there to bear back broken bodies of the brave glorified by the baptism of blood. Again and again the bold ecstasy repeated by other troops, with similar experience, and thickening ridges of the fallen marking the desperate essays.

There we stood for an hour, witnessing five immortal charges. Tears ran down the cheeks of stern men, waiting, almost wishing, to be summoned to the same futile, glorious work. We harkened intensely for the sound of Franklin's guns. Now was heard the exclamation of some veteran commander of ours unable to endure the agony of suspense: "For God's sake, where is Franklin! Where are the sixty thousand that were so quickly to decide this day!'"

We had heard for a little while the boom of guns and a dull roar through the woods below, but all had died away, and a strange boding silence in that quarter desolated our hearts. The rumor came that Meade's division alone had cut through the stubborn lines of Lee's right flank, but unsupported, had been driven back; and thereafter a brave onset by Gibbon's division had met quickly a similar fate—and nothing more seemed attempted; or if so, but in vain.

Now came the call for the reserves! Burnside, despairing of the left and seeing the heroic valor on the right, at last exhausted in unavailing sacrifice, ordered in the Fifth Corps, Griffin's division to lead. First came the silent departure of our first and second brigades, whose course our eyes could not follow. We waited in tremulous expectation. Not in fear, for that has little place in manhood when love and duty summon; but eager to do our best and make the finish. Few words were spoken among officers, however endeared to each other by confidences deepened by such pressure of life on the borders of death as war compels; the sense of responsibility silenced all else. Silence in the ranks, too; one little word, perhaps, telling whom to write to. Griffin gave us a searching, wistful look, not trusting his lips, and we not needing more. Now rang forth the thrilling buglecry, "Third Brigade, to the front!"

OVER THE RIVER AND UP THE HILL

We pushed for the near-by middle pontoon bridge. The enemy's cannon-eers knew the ranges perfectly. The air was thick with the flying, bursting shells; whooping solid shot swept lengthwise our narrow bridge, fortu-nately not yet plowing a furrow through the midst of us, but driving the compressed air so close above our heads that there was an unconquerable instinct to shrink beneath it, although knowing it was then too late. The crowding, swerving column set the pontoons swaying, so that the horses reeled and men could scarcely keep their balance. Forming our line in the lower streets, the men were ordered to unsling knapsacks, and leave them to be cared for by our quartermaster. We began the advance. Two of our regiments had failed to hear the last bugle-calls in the din and roar around, and did not overtake us: we were thus the right of the line. Our other two brigades, we heard, had gone to the relief of Sturgis's division of the Ninth Corps. We were directed straight forward, toward the left of the futile advance we had seen so fearfully cut down. The fences soon compelled us to send our horses back. The artillery fire made havoc. Crushed bodies, severed limbs, were everywhere around, in streets, dooryards, and gardens. Our men began to fall, and were taken up by the faithful surgeons and hospital attendants, who also bring courage to their work.

~

Prior to publication, the Cosmopolitan *editor sent a galley proof of the article for Chamberlain to look over. This version of the piece included a handful of items that were not included in the final publication. This section of the draft manuscript included an encounter with a flock of doves that had somehow failed to escape the tumult, despite their ability to fly. As Chamberlain initially described it,*

> In the black cannon-cloud before us I saw a flock of white-winged doves, scurrying wildly to and fro as if they could find no resting place on earth, nor in the sky. I gazed at them a moment, thinking that if we had wings we perhaps could do no better.*

Whether this account was written as drafted by Chamberlain or was the partial or complete invention of some Hearst scribe intent on selling more magazines, we

---

* Chamberlain, Joshua L. "My Story of Fredericksburg." *Cosmopolitan* magazine galley copy. Special Collections, Raymond H. Fogler Library. University of Maine. Chamberlain Family Papers, 1821–1858.

can only speculate. There is, however, a telling remark, written by Chamberlain in the margins of the draft of the article. Alongside this portion of the text he wrote, "Please omit dog & dove episodes." The Cosmopolitan *editors complied, and the story does not appear in the article's published version.*

Another passage, which was either in the original manuscript or added by editors, described the strange appearance of the Northern Lights during the battle, an unusual occurrence at so far south in latitude, but almost common in the Maine sky back home. In the galley proof sent for his consideration, he marked the section for removal, writing simply "out" in the margin. The passage does not appear in the published article and there is no suggestion as to why Chamberlain decided against including it, though there are many accounts of the phenomenon among soldiers of both armies.

> But it was not all earth's taking. Heaven opened its doors. Our far-away northern sky gave greeting. An aurora borealis of marvelous majesty flashed its high communion: fiery lances and banners of blood and flame, columns of pearly light, garlands and wreaths of gold beckoned a triumphal march over the bridge that spans the worlds. Sleep, stalwart bodies, in the earth you ennobled. Rise, glorious spirits, to your place! Behind that welcoming arch are powers that master forever all that halted you before that stone wall of earthly passion.

The absence of this and a handful of other short passages beside which Chamberlain marked "out" indicates that the author had considerable control over the final content of the article.

Soon we came out in an open field. Immediately, through the murky smoke, we saw to our right a battery swing into position to sweep our front. It opened on us. "God help us now! Colonel, take the right wing; I must lead here!" calmly spoke our brave Colonel Ames to me, and went to the front, into the storm. Now we reached the lines we were to pass for the farther goal. We picked our way amid bodies thickly strewn, some stark and cold some silent with slowly ebbing life; some in sharp agony that must have voice, though unavailing; some prone from sheer exhaustion or by final order of hopeless commander. The living from their close-clung bosom of earth strove to dissuade us: "It's no use, boys; we've tried that. Nothing living can stand there; it's only for the dead!"

On we pushed, up slopes slippery with blood, miry with repeated, unavailing tread. We reached that final crest, before that all-commanding,

countermanding stone wall. Here we exchanged fierce volleys at every disadvantage, until the muzzleflame deepened the sunset red, and all was dark.
We stepped back a little behind the shelter of this forlorn, foremost crest,
and sank to silence, perhaps—such is human weakness—to sleep.

∼

*Chamberlain omitted two anecdotes here that are indicative of the lessons in lead-
ership that he was already learning from Colonel Ames. As the regimental line
approached the upper part of the slope and came into view and range of the enemy
sheltered behind a stone wall, they moved among a mass of troops lying on the
ground. One of them remembered the moment long afterward.*

> When nearly exhausted, a voice from a tall, soldierly-looking colonel
> moving over our prostrate bodies, asked, "What regiment is this?"—
> "The Twenty-Second Massachusetts."—"Where is your commanding
> officer?" Upon Col. Sherwin, who was nearest, being pointed out, he
> said, "Colonel, my regiment will relieve yours firing, if you will move
> them to the rear." We had seen their long, unbroken line, moving
> almost as though at parade, coming across where our route had been
> marked by slaughter, the gaps and holes and tremulous movement of the
> line showing the shock, as the shells and shot raked through. It was Col.
> Adelbert Ames, of the Twentieth Maine, who afterwards commanded a
> division, and later became governor of Mississippi. Our cartridges were
> exhausted, and creeping on all fours to the rear, about twenty feet, his
> line swept over us under a galling fire. They needed no orders. It was
> their first fight, and, under splendid discipline, those Maine boys opened
> a terrific fire. For a moment it seemed as though everybody had taken
> a new lease of life.*

∼

*This personal example of courage and coolness under fire inspired the men and was
among the most important lessons that Lt. Col. Chamberlain learned from Ames,
this time while under fire. It was a lesson he learned well and would make use of on
many battlefields in the coming years.*

*On Chamberlain's part, a private in the regiment remembered years after the
battle an incident that occurred as the regiment was moving up the long slope toward*

---

*   *Henry Wilson's Regiment: History of the Twenty-Second Massachusetts Infantry, the Second Company
Sharpshooters, and the Third Light Battery, in the War of the Rebellion.* Boston: Regimental Association,
1887, pp. 227–28.

the Confederate line. During the advance and in range of the enemy, part of the line of battle encountered a board fence that obstructed their path.

> But this apparently safe position was not gained without a severe test of the men's courage, a high board fence obstructed their advancement and separated the two wings of the advancing line, a perfect storm of bullets pierced and shattered this fence every instant. Orders were given to "down with that fence." It seemed death to any man to touch it, and for a moment the men faltered. "You want *me* to do it do you?" said Col. C seizing the top board and with the assistance of shot and shell wrenched it from its position. It is needless to say such an example resulted in no lack of men to aid in its complete *demolition.*[*]

~

A BIVOUAC OF THE DEAD

It was a cold night. Bitter, raw north winds swept the stark slopes. The men, heated by their energetic and exciting work, felt keenly the chilling change. Many of them had neither overcoat nor blanket, having left them with the discarded knapsack. They roamed about to find some garment not needed by the dead. Mounted officers all lacked outer covering. This had gone back with the horses, strapped to the saddles. So we joined the uncanny quest. Necessity compels, strange uses. For myself it seemed best to bestow my body between two dead men among the many left there by earlier assaults, and to draw another crosswise for a pillow out of the trampled, blood-soaked sod, pulling the flap of his coat over my face to fend off the chilling winds, and, still more chilling, the deep, many-voiced moan that overspread the field. It was heart-rending; it could not be borne. I rose at midnight from my unearthly bivouac, and taking our adjutant for companion went forth to see what we could do for these forsaken sufferers. The deep sound led us to our right and rear, where the fiercest of the fight had held brave spirits too long. As we advanced over that stricken field, the grave, conglomerate monotone resolved itself into its diverse, several elements: some breathing inarticulate agony; some dear home names; some begging for a drop of water; some for a caring word; some praying God for strength to bear; some for life; some for quick death. We did what we

---

[*] George W. Carleton to A. B. Farwell, January 8, 1866. Frost Family Papers, Yale University Library.

could, but how little it was on a field so boundless for feeble human reach! Our best was but to search the canteens of the dead for a draft of water for the dying; or to ease the posture of a broken limb; or to compress a severed artery of fast-ebbing life that might perhaps so be saved with what little skill we had been taught by our surgeons early in learning the tactics of saving as well as of destroying men. It was a place and time for farewells. Many a word was taken for far-away homes that otherwise might never have had one token from the field of the lost. It was something even to let the passing spirit know that its worth was not forgotten here.

Wearied with the sense of our own insufficiency, it was a relief at last to see through the murk the dusky forms of ghostly ambulances gliding up on the far edge of the field, pausing here and there to gather up its precious freight, and the low hovering, half-covered lantern, or blue gleam of a lighted match, held close over a brave, calm face to know whether it were of the living or the dead.

We had taken bearings to lead us back to our place before the stone wall. There were wounded men lying there also, who had not lacked care. But it was interesting to observe how unmurmuring they were. That old New England habit so reluctant of emotional expression, so prompt to speak conviction, so reticent as to the sensibilities—held perhaps as something intimate and sacred—that habit of the blood had its corollary or afterglow in this reticence complaint or murmur under the fearful sufferings and mortal anguish of the battlefield. Yet never have I seen such tenderness as brave men show to comrades when direst need befalls. I trust I show no lack of reverence for gracious spirits nor wrong to grateful memories, when confessing that this tenderness of the stern and strong recalls the Scripture phrase, "passing the love of women."

NIGHT ON THE BATTLEFIELD

Down again into our strange companion-ship of bed! The uncanny quest for covering was still going on around, and coming near. Once a rough but cautious hand lifted the dead man's coatflap from my face, and a wild, ghoullike gaze sought to read whether it was of the unresisting.

All night the winds roared. The things that caught their beat were such as were rooted to earth, or broken and shivered by man's machinery. One sound whose gloomy insistence impressed my mood was the flapping of a loosened window-blind in a forsaken brick house to our right, desolate but for a few daring or despairing wounded. It had a weird rhythm as it swung between the hoarse-answering sash and wall. To my wakened inner sense it struck a chord far deepening the theme of the eternal song of the "old clock on the stairs": "Never—forever; forever—never!" I still seem to hear, in lonely hours with the unforgotten, that dark refrain sounding across the anguished battlefield.

Wakened by the sharp fire that spoke the dawn, as I lifted my head from its restful though strange pillow; there fell out from the breastpocket a much-worn little new Testament written in it the owner's name and home. I could do no less than take this to my keeping, resolved that it should be sent to that home in the sweet valley of the Susquehanna as a token that he who bore it had kept the faith and fought the fight. I may add that sparing mercy allowed the wish to be fulfilled, and this evidence gave the stricken mother's name a place in the list of the nation's remembered benefactors.

Soon came a storm of bullets from front and flank to rout us from our slight shelter in the hollow between the two outermost crest of the manifold assault. This not sufficing, the artillery took up the task, trying to rain shell down upon us and sweep solid shot through our huddled group. We had to lie flat on the earth, and only by careful twisting could any man load and fire his musket against the covered line in front. Before long we saw two or three hundred of the enemy creep out from the right of their stone wall and take advantage of a gullybank where the ground fell away from our left, to get a full flank fire on us.

The situation was critical. We took warrant of supreme necessity. We laid up a breastwork of dead bodies, to cover that exposed flank. Behind this we managed to live through the day. No man could stand up and not be laid down again hard. I saw a man lift his head by the prop of his hands and forearms, and catch a bullet in the middle of his forehead. Such recklessness was forbidden. We lay there all the long day, hearing the dismal "thud" of the bullets into the dead flesh of our life aiding bulwarks. No relief could dare to reach us: reenforcement we did not wish. We saw now and then a staff officer trying to bring orders, and his horse would be shot from under him the moment he reached the crest behind us. We had to take things as they came, and do without the rest.

ORDERED BACK TO FREDERICKSBURG

Night came again, and midway of it the order to remove and take respite within the city. Our wounded were borne to shelter and care back near the pontoon bridge. We got our bodies ready to go, but not our minds. Our dead lay there. We could not take them where we were going, nor could we leave them as they lay. We would bury them in the earth they had made dear. Shallow graves were dug with bayonets and fragments of shell and muskets that strewed the ground. Low headboards, made of broken fence--rails or musket-butts, rudely carved under sheltered match-light, marked each name and home.

We had to pick our way over a field strewn with incongruous ruin; men torn and broken and cut to pieces in every indescribable way, cannon dismounted, guncarriages smashed or overturned, ammunition-chests flung wildly about, horses dead and half-dead still held in harness, accouterments of every sort scattered as by whirlwinds. It was not good for the nerves, that ghastly march, in the lowering night! We were moved to the part of the town first occupied by Sumner's troops, and bivouacked in the streets, on the stone flagging. Little sleep that night, or rest next morning. Troops of all commands were crowded in without pretention of military use or position. Consequently the Confederates began to bombard their own town. Toward night rumors came through prisoners that Stonewall Jackson was coming down from the right upon our huddled mass to crush us where we were or sweep us into the river. No doubt he could have done it. But we afterward learned that Lee did not favor the proposition, not feeling quite sure of the issue. He thought we might fight with our backs to walls as he had seen us fight before them, in the open. Rumor came also that Burnside, in his desperation, had ordered a new assault on the stone-wall front, and proposed to lead his Ninth Corps in person. But, as we afterward learned, Lincoln, hearing of this, wired, forbidding it.

Just after midnight of this miserable day we were summoned—three regiments of us—to set forth on some special service, we knew not what or where, something very serious, we must believe. Some extensive operations were contemplated—we were aware of that from the decided manner and movements of officers and men of all commands. But we were soon assured as to our part. We were bound for the extreme front, to form a picket-line to cover the center of the field while the army was to take some important action. Colonel Ames commanded our line, the regiment coming under my charge. The last order came in low tones, "Hold this ground at all hazards, and to the last!" A strange query crossed our minds: Last of what? No dictionary held that definition. As a general term, this reached the infinite!

REBUKED BY A REBEL PICKET

So we went to work, silently, but intently. Groping about, we laid hold of some picks and spades strewn rather hurriedly around a little to our rear earlier in the night. The men were told to settle themselves into the ground; and let it hold them for a good turn each two, or each for himself, to throw up a little earthwork, elbowlike, behind which the morning's test might be withstood for a while. We were so near the enemy's riflepits that we could hear something of their conversation, from which it appeared that they were about as cautious as we were. We spoke only in whispers. The night was pitch dark. To be sure of the proper direction of our line I had to feel my way along by such tokens as instinct and prudence could provide. Hearing the gravel going at a lively rate a little out of what I thought conformity to instructions, I approached the sound and said in a very confidential tone to the invisible performer,

"Throw to the other side, my man; that's where the danger is!" "Golly!" came back the confident answer, "Don't ye s'pose I know which side them Yanks be? They're right onto us now." I was rebuked and instructed, but must preserve my dignity as a Confederate on "grand rounds." "Dig away then, but keep a right sharp lookout!" I said—then obeyed my own suggestion and "dug away" as calmly as my imperfect lookout would permit.

We were pretty well buried, and braced for the coming dawn, when a strange clatter came up from the left rear, and a gasping voice called, "Where is the commander of these troops?" I acknowledged that responsibility. "Get yourselves out of this as quick as God will let you! The whole army is across the river!" was the message—heard, no doubt, by the whole hostile picket-line. This was a critical moment. Something must be said and done quickly. "Steady in your places, my men!" I ordered. "One or two of you arrest this stampeder! This is a ruse of the enemy! We'll give it to them in the morning!" This was spoken with no suppressed nor hesitating tone, but pitched for the benefit of our astonished neighbors in double darkness in our front. My men caught the keynote of my policy, trusted my discretion, and held themselves quiet. I stepped back to the staff officer, and rebuked him severely for his rashness, pointing out to him the state of things, vexed at having to moderate even my stress of voice. He explained. He had had such a time getting over that field and up to this front line he had almost lost his wits. I could understand this; and told him to follow for himself his message to us, and I would not report his misdemeanor.

HOW WE FINALLY LEFT THE FIELD

I sought out Ames, and we made up a manner of withdrawal: to keep up appearances; to hold the line for a time, with pretended zeal but redoubled caution; then to withdraw under a new form of tactics: even-numbered man to resume his digging and make it lively; every odd-numbered man to step softly to the rear and form line under the second officer of the company; this half of the regiment to move back a hundred yards or so and halt in line of battle, faced to the front, and hold there till the other half, formed in like manner, should come up and pass them to a like distance; then the reciprocal movement to be repeated till we got well to the rear. These tactics proved to be wise, for the enemy, after a short, puzzled hesitation, came out from their entrenchments and followed us up as closely as they deemed safe, the same traits of human nature in them as in us causing a little "nervousness" when moving in darkness and in the presence of an alert enemy, also moving.

Thus we made our way over that stricken field, with stooping walk and muskets at a "trail." It had been a misty night, with fitful rains. Just as our first reach was attained the clouds broke apart in rifts here and there. Through one of these came a sudden gleam from the weird, waning moon, which struck full upon our bright musket-barrels, and revealed us clearly to our watchful pursuers. A bullet or two sang past us. "To the ground, every man of you!" went the quick order, and only a scattering volley sent its baffled greeting over our heads. We had to watch now for favoring clouds.

It was a dreary retreat down those wreck-strewn slopes. It was hard enough to be stumbling over torn-up sods, groups of the dead or forms of the solitary dying, muskets dropped with quick relax, or held fast with death's combustible clutch, swords, bayonets, cartridge-boxes, fragments of everything, everywhere, but when a ghastly gleam of moonlight fell on the pale faces, fixed and stark, and on open eyes that saw not but reflected uttermost things, it sent a shiver through us.

Reaching the pontoon bridge-head just at dawn, we found that the bridge-floor had been muted by sods and brush, that our expected night-tread might not disclose our passing to the pressing foe. We gathered what we could of what had belonged to us, taking along those of our wounded that had not gone before. But the piteous spectacle of others not in our command but belonging to us by the bond of a great brotherhood so moved our large-hearted surgeon, Doctor Hersom, that he begged permission to stay among them. This he did at the cost of being taken prisoner with dire experience of suffering for himself. Sorrowfully but proudly we left him for his ministry of mercy.

So we crossed again that bridge we had passed three days before with strange forebodings but unswerving resolution, little dreaming that we should be put to shame, but now little imputing to ourselves the blame. While waiting for the pontoons some of us had frequently ridden along the bank in full view of the Confederates across the river and through field-glasses studied the construction of their works with curious interest and the natural commonsense inference that we would never be called upon to assault just where Lee had prepared for and wished us.

WHY THE BATTLE WAS LOST

Over the river, then, we marched, and up that bank, whence we now looked back across at Fredericksburg, and saw the green slopes blue with the bodies of our dead. It was raining drearily when I brought the regiment to rest by the dismal wayside. General Hooker came riding slowly by. We had not seen him during the terrible three days. Indeed, he had no business to be where we were. We supposed he and our corps commander, Butterfield, were somewhere controlling and observing their commands. Hooker caught sight of me sitting in the rain leaning back against a tree, and gave kindly greeting. "You've had a hard chance, Colonel; I am glad to see you out of it!" I was not cheerful, but tried to be bright. "It was chance, General; not much intelligent design there!" "God knows I did not put you in!" came the rather crisp reply. "That was the trouble, General. You should have put us in. We were handled in piecemeal, on toastingforks." It was plain talk. And he did not reprove me.

But the general's remark led to wide inferences. It disclosed perhaps the main cause of this great disaster. The commander of the center grand division "did not put his men in!" They were sent by superior order, in detachments, to support other commands, or as a "forlorn hope," at various times and places during the unexpected developments—or rather the almost inevitable accidents of the battle. It should not have been a disaster; Franklin with his 60,000 men should have turned Lee's right; whereas he attacked with only two divisions, and one at a time; and did not follow up with his whole force their splendid initiative.

When Franklin failed, it was rashness to expect Sumner to carry the formidable heights behind the city, made impregnable by Lee's best skill and valor. That front might have been held still under menace while

Sumner, reenforced perhaps by the main body of Hooker's grand division, might have concentrated Lee's left, above the city, and flanked the formidable bastions crowning the heights that entrenched his front with all that earth and manhood could do. That the battle was not fought according to Burnside's intention, and that his plan was mutilated by distrust and disharmony among his subordinate commanders, does not exonerate him, is part of the great trust and place of a chief commander to control reluctant and incongruous elements and to make subordinates and opponents submit to his imperial purpose.

Burnside attempted a vindication somewhat on these lines but too late. He prepared an order removing from command several of his high-ranking but too little subordinate generals, and made ready to prefer charges against them for trial by court-martial. But Lincoln again interposed his commonsense advice, and the matter was passed over.

Not long after, at his own request, Burnside was relieved from command of the army, and magnanimously resumed his place in old Ninth Corps.

− End −

∾

For all of its general descriptions as an utter disaster for Union forces, in relation to other major Civil War battles, Fredericksburg was not the horrible slaughter it is often portrayed as.

Approximately 1 percent of the 122,000-plus Union soldiers present during the three to four days over which fighting occurred were killed. By comparison, twice that, or 2 percent of the Union soldiers present were killed during the Battle of the Wilderness over three days, and 2.5 percent were killed in a single day at the Battle of Antietam. At Gettysburg, federal forces suffered 3 percent killed over three days.

As a regiment, despite having to pick their "way amid bodies thickly strewn," the 20th Maine suffered relatively light casualties with four killed and thirty-five wounded (many listed as "slight"), two of them mortally.

∾

3

THROUGH BLOOD AND
FIRE AT GETTYSBURG

∾

Pleased with the outcome of "My Story of Fredericksburg," Hearst editors asked Chamberlain to draft another article, this one for the fiftieth anniversary of the Battle of Gettysburg. It was slated to run in the June 1913 edition of Hearst's magazine, and the deadline for submission came prior to the publication of the Fredericksburg piece. During the preparation of the Gettysburg article, there was a change in editors at Hearst and with it came a change in style.

Correspondence between Chamberlain and friends after "Through Blood and Fire" appeared in print show that he was very unhappy with the outcome. When friends and fellow comrades mentioned the article, Chamberlain lamented that it "is much curtailed and changed by the insertion of 'connective tissue' by the Editor." "The Hearst editors," he complained to one admirer, "mutilated and 'corrected' my 'Gettysburg' so that I have not tried to get copies of their magazine in which it appeared."*

Lacking a copy of the original manuscript to compare to the final, published article, we will never know exactly which parts of this article come from Chamberlain and which from the imagination of a Hearst editor. There are hints here and there, and these are outlined in the annotations below.

After Fredericksburg, the 20th Maine spent the winter in camp and was not engaged in the disastrous Battle of Chancellorsville in May owing to a smallpox vaccine that infected rather than inoculated the men from the disease. They had recovered well enough by June to join the march northward shadowing Lee's Army of Northern Virginia through its namesake region and into Maryland.

---

* Chamberlain, Joshua L., to Gen. Elliott Dill, 6/12/1913 (MSA). Chamberlain, Joshua L., to Fannie Hardy Eckstrom, 8/28/1913. Special Collections, Raymond H. Fogler Library. University of Maine. Chamberlain Family Papers, 1821–1858.

The story begins with the regiment marching westward from Hanover, Pennsylvania, a village fourteen miles from Gettysburg, where they had been sent in response to a cavalry skirmish the day before. On this side march away from the main body of the army two important things had occurred. First, Joshua Chamberlain returned to the regiment after an absence of about fourteen days to recover from the effects of malarial fever, and possibly dysentery, which many of the men had contracted in a swampy region of Virginia in June. Both illnesses provoke symptoms akin to a bad case of influenza with the latter including unpleasant encounters with diarrhea. When he returned to the unit on July 1, Chamberlain, still not well but aware that a huge battle was imminent, was anxious to take command of his men and relieve Lt. Col. Freeman Conner of the 44th New York Regiment who was serving as the temporary commander during his absence. He also no doubt received the formal notice that he had been promoted to colonel of the regiment, making him the newest such officer in the Army of the Potomac at that moment. He must also have noticed an unfamiliar face in a key role. During his absence, Charles Proctor, the color sergeant, turned up drunk and was arrested. First Sergeant Andrew Tozier in Company I had come over to the regiment from the disbanded 2nd Maine Infantry Regiment six weeks earlier and his service dating back to 1861 made him the senior enlisted man in the unit and thus the next in line to carry the colors.

∿

Nightfall brought us to Hanover, Pennsylvania, and to a halt and it was the evening of the first day of July, 1863. All day we had been marching north from Maryland, searching and pushing out on all roads for the hoped-for collision with [Gen. Robert E.] Lee eagerly, hurriedly, yet cautiously, with skirmishers and flankers out to sound the first challenge, and our main body ready for the call. Fanwise our divisions had been spread out to cover Washington, but more was at stake than the capital city of the Union: there was that important political and international question, the recognition of the Southern Confederacy as independent by France and England.

This recognition, denying the very contentions of the North from the beginning would have been almost fatal to it. And Lee need not win a decided victory in the field to bring about the recognition: his capture and occupation of an important and strategic point in the North would have been enough.

All day, ever and again, we had seen detachments of Lee's cavalry; even as we passed an outlying field to our encampment the red slanting sunlight fell softly across the grim relics of a cavalry fight of the afternoon; the survivors of which had swept on, flying and pursuing.

Worn and famished we stacked arms in camping order, hoping to bivouac beside them, and scampered like madcaps for those two prime factors of a desultory supper—water and fence-rails; for the finding of which the Yankee volunteer has an aptitude which should be ranked among the spiritual intuitions, though in their old-school theology most farmers of our acquaintance were inclined to reckon the aptitude among the carnal appetites of the totally depraved. Some of the forage wagons had now got up, and there was a brief rally at their tail ends for quick justice to be dispensed. But the unregenerate fires had hardly blackened the coffee-dippers, and the hardtack hardly been hammered into working order by the bayonet shanks, when everything was stopped short by whispers of disaster away on the left: the enemy had struck our columns at Gettysburg, and driven it back with terrible loss; [Gen. John F.] Reynolds, the commander, had been killed, and the remnant scarcely able to hold on to the hillsides unless rescue came before morning. These were only rumors flitting owl-like, in the gathering shadows. We could not quite believe them, but they deepened our mood.

TO THE MARCH! ON TO GETTYSBURG!

Suddenly the startling bugle-call from unseen headquarters! "The General!" it rang! "To the march! No moment of delay!"

Word was coming, too. Staff officers dashed from corps, to division, to brigade, to regiment, to battery and the order flew like the hawk, and not the owl. "To Gettysburg!" it said, a forced march of sixteen miles. But what forced it? And what opposed? Not supper, nor sleep, nor sore feet and aching limbs.

In a moment, the whole corps was in marching order; rest, rations, earth itself forgotten; one thought,—to be first on that Gettysburg road. The iron-faced veterans were transformed to boys. They insisted on starting out with colors flying, so that even the night might know what manner of men were coming to redeem the day.

All things, even the most common, were magnified and made mysterious by the strange spell of night. At a turn of the road a staff-officer, with an air of authority, told each colonel as he came up, that [Gen. George B.] McClellan was in command again, and riding ahead of us on the road. Then wild cheers rolled from the crowding column into the brooding sky, and the earth shook under the quickened tread. Now from a dark angle of the roadside came a whisper, whether from earthly or unearthly voice one cannot feel quite sure, that the august form of [George] Washington had been seen that afternoon at sunset riding over the Gettysburg hills. Let no one smile at me! I half believed it myself,—so did the powers of the other world draw nigh!

But there were wayside greetings such as we had never met before. We were in a free state, and among friendly people. All along the road, citizens came out to contemplate this martial array with a certain awe, and greet us with hearty welcome. But, most of all, our dark way was illumined by groups of girls in sweet attire gathered on the embowered lawns of modest homes, with lights and banners and flowers, and stirring songs whose import and effect were quite other than impersonal. Those who were not sisters of the muse of song waved their welcome in the ripple of white handkerchiefs—which token the gallant young gentlemen of the staff were prompt to take as summons to parley, and boldly rode up to meet with soft, half-tone scenes under the summer night: those meetings looked much like proposals for exchange of prisoners, or unconditional surrender. And others still, not daring quite so much, but unable to repress the gracious impulse of giving, offered their silent benediction in a cup of water. And we remembered then with what sanction it was that water had been turned to wine in Cana of Galilee!

OUR BATTLEFIELD, A THIRST FOR BLOOD

Snatching an hour's sleep by the roadside just before dawn, we reached at about seven o'clock in the morning the heights east of Gettysburg, confronting the ground over which the lost battle of the first day had ebbed. After a little, we were moved to the left, across Rock Creek and up the Baltimore Pike to an open field more nearly overlooking the town. On our front and left were the troops of the Eleventh and First Corps; on a commanding height to our right was strongly established the Twelfth Corps of our army. Told to rest awhile, we first resumed the homely repast so sharply interrupted the evening before. Next we stretched ourselves on the ground to make up lost sleep, and rest our feet after a twenty-four hours scarcely broken march, and get our heads level for the coming test.

We knew that a great battle was soon to be fought, a desperate and momentous one. But what much more impressed my mind was the great calm, the uncertainty of overture, and seeming lack of tactical plan for the tremendous issue. We were aware that other troops were coming up, on one side and the other; but we had no means of knowing or judging which side would take the offensive and which the defensive, or where the battle would begin. All the forenoon we had no other intimation as to this, than the order given in an impressive tone to hold ourselves ready to take part in an attack on our right; but whether to be begun by us or the enemy, we neither knew, nor could guess.

We were on Cemetery Hill, the apex of the angle made by an extended ridge, on the right bending sharply back for a mile to end in a lofty wooded crest known as Culp's Hill, and on the left running southerly from the Cemetery, declining somewhat in its course till at the distance of two miles or more it makes an abrupt and rugged rise in a rocky spur, 500 feet high, named Little Round Top.

This was as now the outpost of a steep and craggy peak southward, one hundred and fifty feet higher, terminating the range, named Great Round Top. These landmarks for the whole region near and far, to the west and north especially in a military point of view commanded the entire ground available for a great battle.

Within the wings of this sharp-beaked ridge there entered and met in the town two great thoroughfares, the Baltimore Pike and Taneytown Road, perfectly commanded by the Little Round Top. The latter road opened the direct way to Washington, and in the aspect of affairs was our only practicable line of retreat in case of disaster. Our Second Corps, [Maj. Gen. Winfield S.] Hancock's, had taken position on the ridge, from the Cemetery southerly; and on the extension on this line our Third Corps, [Maj. Gen. Daniel E.] Sickles, was forming—its left, we were told, resting on the northern slope of Little Round Top. This formation indicated a defensive attitude for us, and deepened our confidence in [Maj. Gen. George G.] Meade.

Opposite Cemetery Ridge occupied by us, westerly, something like a mile away, is another ridge, extending from behind the upper limits of the town to nearly opposite the Great Round Top. This is known as Seminary Ridge, so named from the Lutheran Seminary on its northern slope.

[Gen. Richard S.] Ewell's Confederate Corps held the town, and [Gen. Jubal] Early's Division extended northerly and easterly around to the front of Culp's Hill. Their attack, it is curious to observe, was from the north and east—from the direction of York and Hanover—so quickly and completely had Lee turned from his first, and so far successful, attempt to occupy the northern cities, to face the army of the Potomac now threatening their rear. Our orders and expectations still kept us looking anxiously to the right, where the yesterday's battle had left off, and the new one was to begin. But all was as yet uncertain. We were told that General Meade was now conferring with his Corps commanders as to the best point and part for the battle to open. But this symposium was cut short, and a plan of opening announced by a thunder burst of artillery from the rocks and woods away in front of the Round Tops, where we least of all expected it. A crash of musketry followed.

DOUBLE-QUICK TO THE HAVOC OF BATTLE

So the awakening bugle sounded "To the left! At utmost speed!" Down to the left we pushed—the whole Fifth Corps—our brigade nearest and leading; at the double-quick, straight for the strife; not seeking roads, nor minding roughness of ground, thorn-hedges, stone fences, or miry swamps mid-way, earth quaking, sky ablaze, and a deepening uproar as we drew near. We soon saw that our Third Corps was not where we thought—between the Second Corps and the Round Tops—but had been moved forward a mile it seemed, almost to the Emmitsburg Road.

The fight was desperate already. We passed along its rear, first getting a glimpse of the Peach Orchard on the right, where our troops were caught between Hill's Corps on Seminary Ridge and Longstreet's Corps fast arriving on the Emmitsburg Road—and the havoc was terrible. We passed on to the Wheatfield where heroic men standing bright as golden grain were ravaged by Death's wild reapers from the woods. Here we halted to be shown our places. We had a momentary glimpse of the Third Corps left in front of Round Top, and the fearful struggle at the Devil's Den, and [Gen. John B.] Hood's out-flanking troops swarming beyond. Our halt was brief, but our senses alert. I saw our First and Second Brigades go on to the roaring woods, between the Peach Orchard and the Wheatfield.

THE RACE TO LITTLE ROUND TOP

In another instant, a staff officer from [Maj.] General [G.K.] Warren rushed up to find [Maj. Gen. George] Sykes, our Corps Commander, to beg him to send a brigade at least, to seize Little Round Top before the enemy's surging waves should overwhelm it. Other supplications were in the air; calling for aid everywhere. Our [Col. Strong] Vincent, soldierly and self-reliant, hearing this entreaty for Round Top, waited word from no superior, but taking the responsibility ordered us to turn and push for Round Top at all possible speed, and dashed ahead to study how best to place us. We broke to the right and rear, found a rude log bridge over Plum Run, and a rough farm-road leading to the base of the mountain. Here, as we could, we took the double-quick.

Now we learned that Warren, chief engineer of our army, sent by Meade to see how things were going on the left, drawn to Little Round Top by its evident importance, found to his astonishment that it was unoccupied except by a little group of signal-men, earnestly observing the movements over in the region of the Emmitsburg Road beyond the Devil's Den. Warren, to test a surmise, sent word to a battery of ours in position below, to throw a solid shot into a mass of woods in that vicinity. The whir of the shot overhead brought out the glitter of many musket-barrels and bayonets in the slanting sunlight—the revelation of fact, the end of dreams. In a moment more, the fierce attack fell on our Third Corps' left, lashed the Devil's Den into a seething cauldron, leaving free a large Confederate force to sweep past for the base of the Round Tops. They would make short work in taking the height, and Warren did likewise in his call for the race.

~

Gettysburg, more than any other battle of the Civil War, is the subject of ample myths and legends, many of which have little or no basis in fact. The story of Warren ordering a battery of artillery is among those myths. First, Warren had no authority to give orders to a battery of artillery without first getting consent from the commander of its brigade or corps. The battery in question was Smith's Battery—the 4th New York Independent Battery—part of the artillery brigade of the 3rd Corps. Neither Capt. James Smith, the battery commander, nor Capt. George Randolph, commander of the brigade, nor 3rd Corps commander Gen. Dan Sickles ever made mention of receiving such an order. Second, extensive research among surviving accounts and records show no evidence of this order. Third, according to after-action reports from the battery, it had not unlimbered its cannons from its horses at the time Warren's order would have arrived, so it was unable to fire such a round. The source of this story is a letter from Warren to another veteran of the fighting on Little Round Top, but in his next letter, Warren seemed to back off, if not recant, his previous description of events.★

~

★ Warren to Porter Farley, reprinted in Norton, Oliver W., *The Attack and Defense of Little Round Top*, pp. 311–29. On July 24, 1872, Warren seems to regret the description he sent to Farley, asking that "I wrote my letter to you without consulting any notes, and I may not have given the strict order of occurrences in it. If you should wish to publish anything from me, I wish you would let me have time to revise it first."

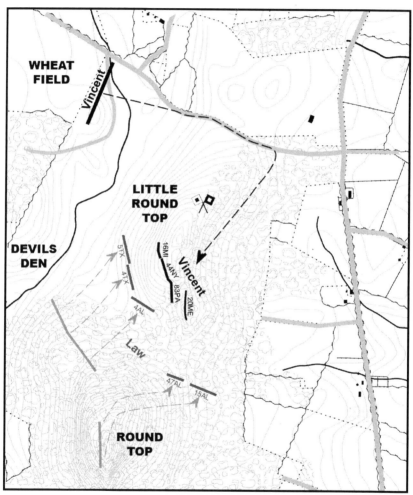

Arrival at Little Round Top—From their original position on the edge of the Wheat Field, the 20th Maine with their brigade marched up the road behind them and over the southern summit of Little Round Top.

Earnestly we scanned that rugged peak which was to be the touch stone of that day's battle. It bore a rough forbidding face, wrinkled with jagged ledges, bearded with mighty boulders; even the smooth spots were strewn with fragments of rock like the play-ground or battleground of giants in the elemental storms of old. Straggling trees wrestled with the rocks for a foot-hold; some were in a rich vein of mould and shot up stark and grim. Altogether it was a strange and solemn place, looking forlorn, and barren now but to be made rich enough soon with precious blood, and far-wept tears.

As we mounted its lower gradient, Longstreet's batteries across Plum Run had us in full view, and turned their whole force upon our path, to sweep the heights free of us till their gray line, now straining towards them, could take them by foot or hand. Shells burst overhead and brought down tree-tops as the hissing fragments fell; or glanced along the shelving ledges and launched splinters of rock to multiply their terrors; solid shot swept close above our heads, their compressed, burning breath driving the men's breath like lead to the bottom of their breasts.

At that fiery moment three brothers of us were riding abreast, and a solid shot driving close past our faces disturbed me. "Boys," I said, "I don't like this. Another such shot might make it hard for mother. Tom, go to the rear of the regiment, and see that it is well closed up! John, pass up ahead and look Out a place for our wounded." Tom, the youngest lieutenant of Company G, was serving as adjutant of the regiment; John, a little older, was sent out by the Christian Commission for this battle, and I had applied for him. We had no surgeon; the old ones were gone, and the new ones not come. So I pressed him into field hospital service, with Chaplain French and the ambulance men, under charge of Hospital Steward [Granville M.] Baker.

∾

*This incident occurred when a fragment of an exploding shell struck the horse of Lt. Rufus Jacklin, adjutant of the 16th Michigan, in the head, killing it instantly and causing it to fall on Jacklin's leg, badly injuring him. Jacklin was riding at the head of his regiment, which placed him directly behind the 20th Maine on the way up Little Round Top.** *

∾

★ Invalid pension record of Major Rufus W. Jacklin, National Archives, Washington, D.C.

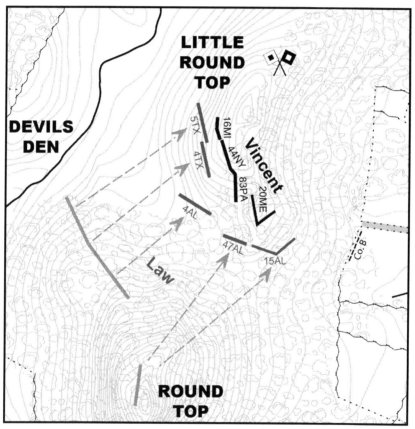

Movements of the 20th Maine and its brigade at Gettysburg.

HOLD THE LINE AT ALL COSTS

As we neared the summit of the mountain, the shot so raked the crest that we had to keep our men below it to save their heads, although this did not wholly avert the visits of tree-tops and splinters of rock and iron, while the boulders and clefts and pitfalls in our path made it seem like the replica of the evil "den" across the sweetly named Plum Run.

~

Describing Little Round Top as a "mountain" is a gross exaggeration. From the lowest point adjacent to the hill to its summit is maximum of one hundred feet. In the area where the 20th Maine fought, it is only forty feet above the plain.

~

Reaching the southern face of Little Round Top, I found Vincent there, with intense poise and look. He said with a voice of awe, as if translating the tables of the eternal law, "I place you here! This is the left of the Union line. You understand. You are to hold this ground at all costs!" I did understand—full well; but had more to learn about costs.

The regiment coming up "right in front" was put in position by a quite uncommon order, "on the right by file into line"; both that we should thus be facing the enemy when we came to a front, and also be ready to commence firing as fast as each man arrived. This is a rather slow style of formation, but this time it was needful.

~

Through many hours of drilling and practice, the men of the regiment had learned to react instinctively to orders and perform maneuvers as depicted in manuals of infantry tactics. Regiments fought in two lines or "ranks," one in front and the other in the rear. Before beginning any marching, the men formed one long line by height, then counted off by twos. Next, the twos would step up so that the single line or rank became two. For obvious reasons, the taller men thus ended up in the rear rank. From this starting point, the regiment always moved "by the right" and came to a front when they reached their destination. In a hurry, a regiment could march "left in front," which meant it was marching backward, or rear first. This could create a problem in combat because the completion of a maneuver or the command of "front" might put the regiment into its fighting position with its back to the enemy. Not an easy thing to remedy quickly. Simply turning each man around was not an option because the taller men in the front row might find it uncomfortable when the first shots were fired. This is what Chamberlain meant when he wrote that the order given would result with the men "facing the enemy when we came to a front." This is also why Chamberlain specified that the regiment arrive "right in front." Other units that fought on the summit of Little Round Top, most notably the 140th New York, arrived on the scene marching "left in front." With no time to perform the required corrective maneuver, they simply charged down into the attacking Texans in front of them, taking the form of a mob rather than a trained fighting unit.

≈

Knowing that we had no supports on the left, I dispatched a stalwart company under the level-headed Captain [Walter G.] Morrill in that direction, with orders to move along up the valley to our front and left, between us and the eastern base of the Great Round Top, to keep within supporting distance of us, and to act as the exigencies of the battle should require.

≈

When Col. Strong Vincent redirected his brigade, which included the 20th Maine, from the edge of the Wheatfield to the summit of Little Round Top, they marched in the order in which they had been arrayed when in line of battle. This placed the 16th Michigan behind the 20th Maine, as confirmed by the death of Adjutant Jacklin's horse. Standard practice upon arrival on a field of battle was to dispatch a group of men as skirmishers out in front of the regiment several dozen yards to act as an early warning system if the enemy appeared.

When Capt. Morrill followed Chamberlain's orders to deploy his company as skirmishers, he marched forward and slightly leftward believing he would hook up with the right end of the 16th Michigan's skirmishers and extend the brigade skirmish line from there over to the unit on the 20th's right, the 83rd Pennsylvania. Unknown to Chamberlain or Morrill, Col. Vincent had redirected the 16th Michigan from the 20th's left around to the far right of the brigade position. Morrill never located the 16th's skirmishers and ended up just barely missing the approach of the oncoming Alabamians. When he heard the firing begin behind him and to his right, Morrill ordered his men to take position behind a nearby stone wall where they listened to, but did not take part in, the fighting that occurred just over one hundred heavily wooded yards in front of them.

≈

DO DUTY OR BE SHOT

The Twentieth Maine Regiment had 358 men equipped for duty in the ranks with twenty-eight officers. They were all well-seasoned soldiers, and what is more, well-rounded men, body and brain. One somewhat important side-note must have place here, in order properly to appreciate the mental and moral attitude of the men before us. One hundred and twenty of these men from the Second Maine were recruits, whom some recruiting officer had led into the belief that they should be discharged with their regiment at the end of its term of service. In their enthusiasm they had not noticed that they were signing enlistment papers for "three years of the war"; and when they had been held in the field after the discharge of the regiment they had refused to do military duty, and had been sequestered in a prisoners' camp as mutineers, waiting court-martial. The exigency of our movement the last of May had not permitted this semi-civil treatment; and orders from the Secretary of War had directed me to take these men up on my rolls and put them to duty. This made it still harder for them to accept, as they had never enlisted in this regiment. However, they had been soon brought over to me under guard of the One Hundred and Eighteenth Pennsylvania, with fixed bayonets; with orders to me to take them into my regiment and "make them do duty, or shoot them down the moment they refused"; these had been the very words of the Corps Commander in person. The responsibility, I had thought, gave me some discretionary power. So I had placed their names on our rolls, distributed them by groups, to equalize companies, and particularly to break up the "esprit de corps" of banded mutineers. Then I had called them together and pointed out to them the situation, that they could not be entertained as civilian guests by me; that they were by authority of the United States on my rolls as soldiers, and I should treat them as soldiers should be treated; that they should lose no rights by obeying orders, and would see what could be done for their claim. It is pleasant to record that all but one or two had gone back manfully to duty, to become some of the best soldiers in the regiment, as I was to prove this very day.

~

This description of the transfer of the 2nd Maine holdouts is somewhat similar to the military records created at the time. While all 173 soldiers were officially transferred on paper from the roll of their old regiment to the 20th Maine on May 20, 1863, the 20th's Consolidated Morning Reports show that the physical movement happened in a piecemeal fashion probably, as Chamberlain describes, so as to break up any resistance to service. The first group of 2nd Mainers, sixty-nine men in all, physically arrived in the 20th on May 26, 1863. As Chamberlain described, these were divided on the rolls among nine companies from five to nine men each.

Nine more arrived on May 27 and another two on May 28. On May 30, twenty-six arrived "under arrest," the next day another thirty-one "under guard." On June 9, another thirty arrived, and sixteen more on June 11. Chamberlain may have spoken with those who arrived under guard and arrest at the end of May, but there was clearly no grand, emotional speech as was fictionalized in Michael Shaara's 1974 novel, The Killer Angels, *and portrayed in the 1993 movie* Gettysburg, *based upon it.**

~

NOT A MAN WAVERS NOW

The exigency was great. I released the pioneers and provost guard alto-gether, and sent them to their companies. All but the drummer boys and hospital attendants went into the ranks. Even the cooks and servants not liable to such service asked to go in. Others whom I knew to be sick or footsore, and had given a pass to "fall out" on the forced marches of the day and night before, came up, now that the battle was on, dragging themselves along on lame and bleeding feet, finding their regiment with the sagac-ity of the brave, and their places where need is greatest and hearts truest. "Places?" Did any of these heroic men ever leave them?—although for all too many we passed their names at evening roll all thereafter, with only the hearts answer, "Here forever!"

Our line looked towards the Great Round Top, frowning above us, not a gunshot away, and raising grave thoughts of what might happen if the enemy should gain foothold there, even if impracticable for artillery.

We had enough of that, as it was. For the tremendous cannonade from across the Plum Run gorge was still pounding the Little Round Top crests; happily, not as yet striking my line, which it would have enfilade if it got the range.

The other regiments of the brigade were forming on our right; the Eighty-third Pennsylvania, the Forty-fourth New York, and the Sixteenth

---

* 20th Maine Infantry Consolidated Morning Reports, single bound volume. Adjutant Gen-eral's Collection, Maine State Archives.

Michigan. I was observing and meditating as to the impending and the possible, when something of the real was substituted by a visit from Colonel
[James C.] Rice [commander of the 44th New York]. He thought it would
be profitable for us to utilize these few minutes by going to the clearer
space on the right of his regiment to take a look at the aspect of things in
the Plum Run valley—the direction of the advance on our front. It was a
forewarning indeed. The enemy had already turned the Third Corps left,
the Devil's Den was a smoking crater, the Plum Run gorge was a whirling
maelstrom; one force was charging our advanced batteries near the Wheatfield; the flanking force was pressing past the base of the Round Tops; all
rolling towards us in tumultuous waves.

It was a stirring, not to say, appalling sight; here a whole battery of
shot and shell cutting a ragged chasm through a serried mass, flinging men
and horses like drift aside; there, a rifle volley at close range, with reel-
ing shock, hands tossed in air, muskets dropped with death's quick relax,
or clutched with last, convulsive energy, men falling like grass before the
scythe—others with manhood's proud calm and rally; there, a little group
kneeling above some favorite officer slain,—his intense spirit still animat-
ing the fiery steed pressing headlong with empty saddle to the van; here,
a defiant regiment of ours, broken, slaughtered, captured; or survivors of
both sides crouching among the rocks for shelter from the terrible crossfire
where there is no rear! But all advancing—all the frenzied force, victors and
vanquished, each scarcely knowing which—surging and foaming towards
us; death around, be-hind, before, and madness everywhere!

Yes, brave Rice! it was well for us to see this; the better to see it
through. A look into each other's eyes; without a word, we resumed our
respective places.

∽

*This passage illustrates one of two things. It may be part of the "mutilation" and
adding of "connective tissue" to the original draft that Chamberlain blamed on
Hearst's editors. It may also be a classic example of Chamberlain's tendency to
unnecessarily exaggerate details that have no bearing on the story overall. When it
came to the actions of his men or the details of the combat he engaged in person-
ally, Chamberlain's descriptions tended to be accurate—factually supported by other
accounts and evidence. However, when he wrote about more distant events that were
inconsequential to his own experience or the outcome of the fighting, he tended to
engage in what one contemporary critic of his described as "vain gloriousness" or
inflating combat-associated danger or harm with vivid descriptive phrases such as "a*

defiant regiment of ours, broken, slaughtered, captured," or "a whole battery of shot and shell cutting a ragged chasm through a serried mass, flinging men and horses like drift aside." These things did not occur in the region of Devil's Den within clear view of the southern slope of Little Round Top, and whether they were the invention of Chamberlain or a Hearst editor, they play no role in the story that the article is portraying, except as general tone-setting visual imagery.

∾

A LULL, THEN THE CRASH OF HELL

Ten minutes had not passed. Suddenly the thunder of artillery and crash of iron that had all the while been roaring over the Round Top crests stopped short.

We understood this, too. The storming lines, that had swept past the Third Corps' flank, had got up the base of Little Round Top, and under the range and reach of their guns. They were close upon us among the rocks, we knew, unseen, because so near. In a minute more came the roll of musketry. It struck the exposed right center of our brigade.

Promptly answered, repulsed, and renewed again and again, it soon reached us, still extending. Two brigades of Hood's Division had attacked—Texas and Alabama. The Fourth Alabama reached our right, the Forty-seventh Alabama joined and crowded in, but gradually, owing to their echelon advance. Soon seven companies of this regiment were in our front. We had all we could stand. My attention was sharply called, now here, now there. In the thick of the fight and smoke, Lieutenant [James H.] Nichols, a bright officer near our center, ran up to tell me something queer was going on in his front, behind those engaging us.

∾

Those who read Civil War battle narratives often struggle with the meaning of the words "our" and "we" in these contexts. Sometimes "we" meant the entire army, other times, it could refer to a regiment or company. Often the words changed in meaning more than once in the description of a single battle. In reality, only one and a half of the Alabama regiments, about 500 or so men, attacked the 20th's regimental line. The entire 15th Alabama on their far left and the undersized 47th Alabama to their front. Because this body of troops had climbed "Big Round Top" on their way to the scene, they had become separated from the rest of the Confederate

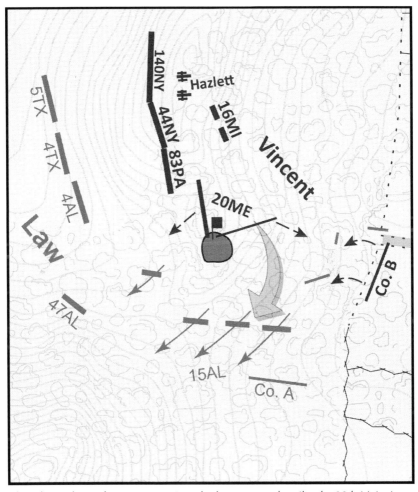

Though not the perfect representation, the best way to describe the 20th Maine's charge was as a wheeling motion of the left wing toward their right.

line, specifically the 4th Alabama Infantry, by more than a hundred yards. When he wrote that the 4th "reached our right" he meant the brigade's right. When he said that seven companies of the 47th Alabama "were in our front," he meant the 20th Maine's front.

In 1878, Col. William C. Oates, commander of the 15th Alabama who also had some authority of the partial 47th Alabama on his left, mistakenly wrote in a widely circulated article that he entered the fight with "644 men and 42 officers," in just the 15th Alabama, of which, "I lost 343 men and 19 officers." These numbers remained the accepted public record and were repeated often in other descriptions of the battle, including the wording on the 20th Maine's Little Round Top monument. The fact that they are mistaken and grossly inflated, did not enter the public realm until Oates published a book in 1905 in which he explained, "In the hasty manner of writing my report I took as a basis of the strength of my regiment its last muster before we began the march to Pennsylvania. I also wrote the article after the war on the same basis, which was a mistake." With thirty-seven more years to ponder his experience at Gettysburg, Oates reckoned that less than 400 men of his regiment attacked the 20th Maine, making the odds, once the 47th Alabama made its very early exit from the fight, about equal. This has not stopped chroniclers of the battle from 1863 to today from exaggerating the numerical odds to three to one and as many as ten to one in Oates's favor.

The mention of Lt. James Nichols is interesting as he was a personal acquaintance of Chamberlain's, having been a prominent tailor in the Colonel's hometown of Brunswick, Maine, before the war. Nichols was unusually brave but a hard man to like, apparently by his own preference. He rarely drank alcohol, but when he did, he made up in volume what he lacked in frequency. Less than a month earlier, Col. Adelbert Ames had placed Nichols under arrest as the result of a multi-day bender. In December, Chamberlain again placed Nichols under arrest for the same offense and later tried to facilitate a transfer for him to the cavalry but he instead resigned his commission and left the army in the early part of 1864. Chamberlain's mention of him here may have been a moment of nostalgia, as Nichols died of alcohol-induced kidney disease in 1884.*

~

* Pension record of James H. Nichols, National Archives, Washington, D.C. Chamberlain to Gov. Samuel Cony, 3/10/1864. Records of the Adjutant General of Maine, Civil War Collection, 20th Maine Regimental Correspondence. Maine State Archives. Nichols's death certificate lists his cause of death as "Chronic Inter[stitial] Nephritis"—a loss of kidney function specifically related to chronic alcohol abuse.

THE GRAY IS FLANKING US!

I sprang forward, mounted a great rock in the midst of his [Nichols's] company line, and was soon able to resolve the "queer" impression into positive knowledge. Thick groups in gray were pushing up along the smooth dale between the Round Tops in a direction to gain our left flank.

There was no mistaking this. If they could hold our attention by a hot fight in front while they got in force on that flank, it would be bad for us and our whole defence. How many were coming we could not know. We were rather too busy to send out a reconnaissance. If a strong force should gain our rear, our brigade would be caught as by a mighty shears-blade, and be cut and crushed. What would follow it was easy to foresee. This must not be. Our orders to hold that ground had to be liberally interpreted. That front had to be held, and that rear covered.

Something must be done,—quickly and coolly. I called the captains and told them my tactics: To keep the front at the hottest without special regard to its need or immediate effect, and at the same time, as they found opportunity, to take side steps to the left, coming gradually into one rank, file-closers and all.

∽

This involved thinning the usual two-deep battle line into one single "rank" and stretching the regiment into a weaker but longer line to cover more ground. File closers in Civil War tactics were higher ranking noncommissioned officers and lieutenants whose normal position was just behind the rear rank. These men closed holes created by casualties by stepping up into empty spaces that appeared in the regimental line during the fighting.

∽

Then I took the colors with their guard and placed them at our extreme left, where a great boulder gave token and support; thence bending back at a right angle the whole body gained ground leftward and made twice our original front. And were not so long doing it. This was a difficult movement to execute under such a fire, requiring coolness as well as heat. Of rare quality were my officers and men. I shall never cease to admire and honor them for what they did in this desperate crisis.

∽

It is on this great boulder that the surviving veterans placed the 20th Maine's monument in 1884.

~

Now as an important element of the situation, let our thoughts turn to what was going on meanwhile to the right of us. When [Gen. G. K.] Warren [Chief Engineer of the Army of the Potomac] saw us started for Little Round Top, looking still intently down, he saw Hood's two brigades breaking past the Third Corps' left and sweeping straight for Little Round Top. Then he flew down to bring reinforcement for this vital place and moment. He came upon the One Hundred and Fortieth New York, of [Gen. Stephen] Weed's Brigade of our Second Division, just going in to [Third Corps commander Gen. Daniel] Sickles' relief, and dispatched it headlong for Round Top. Weed was to follow, and [Gen. Romeyn B.] Ayres' whole division—but not yet.

Warren also laid hold of [Lt. Charles E.] Hazlett, with his battery, D of the Fifth Regulars, and sent him to scale those heights—if in the power of man so to master nature.

~

Warren was especially fortunate. In the midst of this crisis, he descended Little Round Top by the rearward logging trail and came immediately upon the 140th New York Infantry and its commander, Col. Patrick O'Rorke. Rather than engaging in the usual delays associated with orders from a general not within the chain of command of an officer, O'Rorke reacted immediately. This was owing to the fact that Warren was the previous commander of this brigade (2nd Brigade, 1st Division, 5th Corps) that included the 140th New York and, as such, O'Rorke was familiar with him on sight. Without taking time to load rifles or reverse their marching order (they were marching "left in front") O'Rorke and his 500 New Yorkers started immediately up the path toward the summit.

~

Meantime the tremendous blow of the Fourth and Fifth Texas struck the right of our brigade, and our Sixteenth Michigan reeled and staggered back under the shock. Confusion followed. Vincent felt that all was lost unless the very gods should intervene. Sword aloft and face aflame, he rushed in among the broken companies in desperate effort to rally them, man by man.

By sheer force of his superb personality he restored a portion of his line, and was urging up the rest "Don't yield an inch now, men, or all is lost!" he cried, when an answering volley scorched the very faces of the men, and Vincent's soul went up in a chariot of fire. In that agonizing moment, came tearing up the One Hundred and Fortieth New York, gallant [Col. Patrick H.] O'Rorke at the head. Not waiting to load a musket or form a line, they sprang forward into that turmoil. Met by a withering volley that killed its fine young colonel and laid low many of his intrepid officers and a hundred of his men, this splendid regiment, as by a providence we may well call divine; saved us all in that moment of threatened doom.

∾

In reality, Vincent's soul did not then go up in a chariot of fire. He was wounded, taken rearward to a nearby farmhouse which medical personnel had commandeered as a field hospital. The colonel died as a result of the wounds five days later.

∾

To add a tragic splendor to this dark scene, in the midst of it all, the indomitable Hazlett was trying to get his guns—ten-pounder rifled Parrotts—up to a working place on the summit close beyond. Finally he was obliged to take his horses entirely off, and lift his guns by hand and handspike up the craggy steep, whence he launched death and defiance wide and far around.

∾

"Ten-pounder rifled Parrots" were rifled cannon invented in 1860 by West Point graduate Robert Parker Parrott who became superintendent of the West Point Foundry in Cold Spring, New York. Recognized by its three-inch muzzle and distinctive, reinforcing band around the back end, this gun fired a ten-pound shot more than a mile with considerable accuracy. Despite the enormous challenge of pushing these guns up the steep eastern slope of Little Round Top, Hazlett got two of his six guns into action before the fighting subsided. These were of no use against the Texans then attacking the summit of the hill because their muzzles could not be aimed in a downward direction toward the enemy when fired. However, the booming of the guns had a disheartening effect on the assaulting force and an encouraging one on the Union troops.

∾

The roar of all this tumult reached us on the left, and heightened the intensity of our resolve. Meanwhile the flanking column worked around to our left and joined with those before us in a fierce assault, which lasted with increasing fury for an intense hour. The two lines met and broke and mingled in the shock. The crush of musketry gave way to cuts and thrusts, grapplings and wrestlings. The edge of conflict swayed to and fro, with wild whirlpools and eddies. At times I saw around me more of the enemy than of my own men: gaps opening, swallowing, closing again with sharp convulsive energy; squads of stalwart men who had cut their way through us, disappearing as if translated. All around, strange, mingled roar—shouts of defiance, rally, and desperation; and underneath, murmured entreaty and stifled moans; gasping prayers, snatches of Sabbath song, whispers of loved names; everywhere men torn and broken, staggering, creeping quivering on the earth, and dead faces with strangely fixed eyes staring stark into the sky. Things which cannot be told—nor dreamed.

How men held on, each one knows, not I. But manhood commands admiration. There was one fine young fellow, who had been cut down early in the fight with a ghastly wound across his forehead, and who I had thought might possibly be saved with prompt attention. So I had sent him back to our little field hospital, at least to die in peace. Within a half-hour, in a desperate rally I saw that noble youth amidst the rolling smoke as an apparition from the dead, with bloody bandage for the only covering of his head, in the thick of the fight, high-borne and pressing on as they that shall see death no more. I shall know him when I see him again, on whatever shore!

THE COLORS STAND ALONE

So, too, another. In the very deepest of the struggle our shattered line had pressed the enemy well below their first point of contact, and the struggle to regain it was fierce, I saw through a sudden rift in the thick smoke our colors standing alone. I first thought some optical illusion imposed upon me. But as forms emerged through the drifting smoke, the truth came to view. The cross-fire had cut keenly; the center had been almost shot away, only two of the color-guard had been left, and they fighting to fill the whole space; and in the center, wreathed in battle smoke, stood the Color-Sergeant, Andrew Tozier. His color-staff planted in the ground at his side, the upper part clasped in his elbow, so holding the flag upright, with musket and cartridges seized from the fallen comrade at his side he was defending his sacred trust in the manner of the songs of chivalry. It was a stirring picture—its import still more stirring.

~

The presence of Tozier in this part of the story may be the result of a post-war relationship between the two men rather than anything that occurred on July 2, 1863. To be sure, the color bearer was among the bravest men in the regiment, or his previous unit the 2nd Maine. Wounded multiple times, including once in the head, Tozier refused to accept a discharge for disability and continued to be present in the thick of the fight at every opportunity. When his enlistment finally expired, he returned to Maine and engaged in a crime spree that involved several counties. It took five years, but he was eventually tried, convicted, and sentenced to five years in the state prison. He served very little of that time, however, before receiving a full pardon from the governor of Maine, who just happened to be his former commander. Chamberlain not only freed Tozier but took him and his wife into his home and helped set him on a straight path. In 1898 Chamberlain advocated successfully for a Medal of Honor for Tozier based on his service at Gettysburg.

~

That color must be saved, and that center too. I sent first to the regiment on our right for a dozen men to help us here, but they could not spare a man. I then called my young brother, Tom, the adjutant, and sent him forward to close that gap somehow; if no men could be drawn from neighboring companies, to draw back the salient angle and contract our center. The fire down there at this moment was so hot I thought it impossible for him to get there alive; and I dispatched immediately after him Sergeant (Reuel) Thomas whom I had made a special orderly, with the same instructions. It needed them both; and both came back with personal proofs of the perilous undertaking. It was strange that the enemy did not seize that moment and point of weakness. Perhaps they saw no weakness. Perhaps it was awe or admiration that held them back from breaking in upon that sublime scene.

When that mad carnival lulled,—from some strange instinct in human nature and without any reason in the situation that can be seen—when the battling edges drew asunder, there stood our little line, groups and gaps, notched like saw-teeth, but sharp as steel, tempered in infernal heats like a magic sword of the Goths. We were on the appointed and entrusted line. We had held ground—flat "at all costs!"

But sad surprise! It had seemed to us we were all the while holding our own, and had never left it. But now that the smoke dissolved, we saw our dead and wounded all out in front of us, mingled with more of the enemy. They were scattered all the way down to the very feet of the baffled hostile line now rallying in the low shrubbery for a new onset. We could not wait for this. They knew our weakness now. And they were gathering force. No place for tactics now! The appeal must be to primal instincts of human nature!

~

The nature of this passage heavily implies that it was significantly altered by a Hearst editor. Shortly before the charge down the slope, Holman Melcher, an officer in the color company came over to Chamberlain and asked if he could move his line of battle forward a few steps to cover some wounded lying in front of it. It appears that this exchange was exaggerated so that the wounded lay all the way down the hill and the regiment undertook a major maneuver for the purpose of recovering them. There is no record of such a maneuver, however.

~

DOWN THE DEATH-STREWN SLOPE!

"Shall they die there, under the enemy's feet, and under your eyes?" Words like those brokenly uttered, from heart to heart, struck the stalwart groups holding together for a stand, and roused them to the front quicker than any voice or bugle of command. These true-hearted men but a little before buffeted back and forth by superior force, and now bracing for a dubious test, dashed down the death-strewn slope into the face of the rallied and recovering foe, and hurled them, tore them from above our fallen as the tiger avenges its young. Nor did they stop till they had cleared the farthest verge of the field, redeemed by the loving for the lost—the brave for the brave.

Now came a longer lull. But this meant, not rest, but thought and action. First, it was to gather our wounded, and bear them to the sheltered lawn for saving life, or peace in dying; the dead, too that not even our feet should do them dishonor in the coming encounter. Then—such is heavenly human pity—the wounded of our Country's foes; brothers in blood for us now, so far from other caring; borne to like refuge and succor by the drummer-boys who had become angels of the field.

In this lull I took a turn over the dismal field to see what could be done for the living, in ranks or recumbent; and came upon a manly form and face I well remembered. He was a sergeant earlier in the field of Antietam and of Fredericksburg; and for refusing to perform some menial personal service for a bullying quartermaster in winter camp, was reduced to the ranks by a commander who had not carefully investigated the case. It was a degradation, and the injustice of it rankled in his high-born spirit. But his well-bred pride would not allow him to ask for justice as a favor. I had kept this in mind, for early action. Now he was lying there, stretched on an open front where a brave stand had been made, face to the sky, a great bullet-hole in the middle of his breast, from which he had loosened the clothing to ease his breathing, and the rich blood was pouring in a stream. I bent down over him. His face lightened; his lips moved. But I spoke first, "My dear boy, it has gone hard with you. You shall be cared for!" He whispered, "Tell my mother I did not die a coward!" It was the prayer of home-bred manhood poured out with his life-blood. I knew and answered him, "You die a sergeant. I promote you for faithful service and noble courage on the field of Gettysburg!"

This was all he wanted. No word more. I had him borne from the field, but his high spirit had passed to its place. It is needless to add that as soon as a piece of parchment could be found after that battle, a warrant was made out promoting George Washington Buck to sergeant in the terms told him; and this evidence placed the sad, proud mother's name on the rolls of the Country's benefactors.

MY LIFE HANGS ON AN IMPULSE

As for myself, so far I had escaped. How close an escape I had I did not know till afterwards. I think I may mention here, as a psychological incident, that some years after the war, I received a letter written in a homely but manly style by one subscribing himself "a member of the Fifteenth Alabama," in these words:

> Dear Sir: I want to tell you of a little passage in the battle of Round Top, Gettysburg, concerning you and me, which I am now glad of. Twice in that fight I had your life in my hands. I got a safe place between two big rocks, and drew bead fair and square on you. You were standing in the open behind the center of your line, full exposed. I knew your rank by your uniform and your actions, and I thought it a mighty

good thing to put you out of the way. I rested my gun on the rock and took steady aim. I started to pull the trigger, but some queer notion stopped me. Then I got ashamed of my weakness and went through the same motions again. I had you, perfectly certain. But that same queer something shut right down on me. I couldn't pull the trigger, and gave it up, that is, your life. I am glad of it now, and hope you are.

Yours truly.

I thought he was that, and answered him accordingly, asking him to come up North and see whether I was worth what he missed. But my answer never found him, nor could I afterwards.

∾

Chamberlain kept every letter, order, and record that he ever received, and these remain held in numerous archival collections across the country. In none of these collections is there an original, copy, or even mention of this letter describing this important scene. This, of course, suggests it was made up out of whole cloth by a Hearst editor. A somewhat similar letter that does exist among the collections of Chamberlain papers came from a friend who had been traveling in Alabama in 1903 and found himself in a hotel owned by W. R. Painter, a veteran of the 15th Alabama. Learning that his guest was from Maine, the hotelier told him the story of his service at Gettysburg, how he clearly identified Chamberlain as the enemy commander and fired a shot directly at him. Just as he did, "Chamberlain's life was only saved by the act of a private who sprang in front of the Colonel and received the shot himself; killing him." Though there is no direct evidence connecting the two stories, it is not difficult to imagine Chamberlain describing the existing letter in his initial draft, only to have a Hearst editor read it and improve it by addition of mutilation and connective tissue.*

∾

THE LAST CARTRIDGE AND BARE STEEL

The silence and the doubt of the momentary lull were quickly dispelled. The formidable Fifteenth Alabama, repulsed and as we hoped dispersed,

---

* Heath, Herbert W., to Joshua Chamberlain, 2/7/1903. Maine Historical Society. The letter referenced W. R. Painter, a veteran of the 15th Alabama who owned Merchants Hotel in Ozark, Alabama.

now in solid and orderly array—still more than twice our numbers—came rolling through the fringe of chaparral on our left. No dash; no yells; no demonstrations for effect; but settled purpose and determination! We opened on them as best we could. The fire was returned, cutting us to the quick. The Forty-Seventh Alabama had rallied on our right.

According to numerous Alabama accounts, the 47th Alabama was engaged in front of the 20th Maine and the 83rd Pennsylvania for only the first few minutes of the initial attack before it fell back out of the fight for the duration. Its list of casualties seems to confirm its limited participation with just six men killed and forty-six wounded, many of these described as "slightly." This, and the nature of the gap between the 15th and 47th and the rest of the brigade, is also borne out by the relatively light casualties reported by the 83rd Pennsylvania that lost fifty-five men (ten killed) in contrast to the 20th Maine's loss of 129, forty of whom were killed or mortally wounded. On the 83rd's right, the 44th New York lost twenty-six killed.

We were enveloped in fire, and sure to be overwhelmed in fact when the great surge struck us. Whatever might be otherwise, what was here before us was evident; these far outnumbering, confident eyes, yet watching for a sign of weakness. Already I could see the bold flankers on their right darting Out and creeping and crawling like under the smoke to gain our left, thrown back as it was. It was for us, then, once for all. Our thin line was broken, and the enemy were in rear of the whole Round Top defense—infantry, artillery, humanity itself—with the Round Top and the day theirs.

Now, too, our fire was slackening; our last rounds of shot had been fired; what I had sent for could not get to us. I saw the faces of my men one after another, when they had fired their last cartridge, turn anxiously towards mine for a moment; then square to the front again. To the front for them lay death; to the rear what they would die to save. My thought was running deep. I was combining the elements of a "forlorn hope," and had just communicated this to Captain Ellis Spear of the wheeling flank, on which the initiative was to fall. Just then—so will a little incident fleck a brooding cloud of doom with a tint of human tenderness—brave, warm-hearted Lieutenant [Holman S.] Melcher, of the Color Company,

---

★ Desjardin, *Stand Firm Ye Boys from Maine*, pp. 203–5.

whose Captain and nearly half his men were down, came up and asked if he might take his company and go forward and pick up one or two of his men left wounded on the field, and bring them in before the enemy got too near. This would be a most hazardous move in itself and in this desperate moment, we could not break our line. But I admired him. With a glance, he understood, I answered, "Yes, sir, in a moment! I am about to order a charge!"

Not a moment was to be lost! Five minutes more of such a defensive, and the last roll-call would sound for us! Desperate as the chances were, there was nothing for it, but to take the offensive. I stepped to the colors. The men turned towards me. One word was enough,— "BAYONET!"— It caught like fire, and swept along the ranks. The men took it up with a shout,—one could not say, whether from the pit, or the song of the morning star! It were vain to order "Forward." No mortal could have heard it in the mighty hosanna that was winging the sky. Nor would he want to hear. There are things still as of the first creation, "whose seed is in itself." The grating clash of steel in fixing bayonets told its own story; the color rose in front; the whole line quivered for the start; the edge of the left-wing rippled, swung, tossed among the rocks, straightened, changed curve from cimetar to sickle-shape; and the bristling archers swooped down upon the serried host—down into the face of half a thousand! Two hundred men!

~

It is important to note here that in his 1905 book, Colonel Oates of the 15th Alabama described this moment very differently. He wrote that he entered the fight with less than 500 men and had just given them an order to prepare to retreat back in the direction they had come in hopes of taking and holding Big Round Top. This book, and the records of the 20th Maine show that more than 160 men of the 15th ended up killed, wounded, or captured by the end of the fight, leaving Oates with not much more than 200 men still in the fight.

~

It was a great right wheel. Our left swung first. The advancing foe stopped, tried to make a stand amidst the trees and boulders, but the frenzied bayonets pressing through every space, forced a constant settling to the rear. Morrill with his detached company and the remnants of our valorous sharpshooters, who had held the enemy so long in check on the slopes of the Great Round Top, now fell upon the flank of the retiring crowd, and it turned to full retreat, some up amidst the crags of Great Round Top, but most down the smooth vale towards their own main line on Plum Run. This tended to mass them before our center. Here their stand was more stubborn. At the first dash the commanding officer I happened to confront, coming on fiercely, sword in one hand and big navy revolver in the other, fires one barrel almost in my face; but seeing the quick saber-point at his throat, reverses arms, gives sword and pistol into my hands and yields himself prisoner. I took him at his word, but could not give him further attention. I passed him over into the custody of a brave sergeant at my side, to whom I gave the sword as emblem of his authority, but kept the pistol with its loaded barrels, which I thought might come handy soon, as indeed it did.

∾

The officer was Lt. Robert Wicker and Chamberlain remembered later that the pistol had four unfired rounds still inside.

∾

Ranks were broken; many retired before us somewhat hastily; some threw their muskets to the ground—even loaded: sunk on their knees, threw up their hands, calling out, "We surrender. Don't kill us!" As if we wanted to do that! We kill only to resist killing. And these were manly men, whom we would befriend, and by no means kill, if they came our way in peace and good will.

∾

Whether this is a Hearst comment for the benefit of their Southern readers or, less likely, a nostalgic reminiscence by Chamberlain, this passage reflects the spirit of reunion and remembrance that was common among the survivors of the war in the early part of the twentieth century. It was not the feeling among the men of the 20th Maine in 1863 having just endured more than an hour of horrific combat while their comrades fell around them. There are no contemporary accounts expressing benevolence and sympathy toward their enemy on that day from among the Maine men.

∾

Charging right through and over these, we struck the second line of the Forty-seventh Alabama doing their best to stand, but offering little resistance. Their Lieutenant-Colonel as I passed—and a fine gentleman was Colonel [Michael J.] Bulger—introduced himself as my prisoner, and as he was wounded, I had him cared for as best we could. Still swinging to the right as a great gate on its hinges, we swept the front clean of assailants. We were taking in prisoners by scores—more than we could hold, or send to the rear, so that many made final escape up Great Round Top.

Half way down to the throat of the vale I came upon Colonel [Robert M.] Powell of the Fifth Texas, a man of courtly bearing, who was badly wounded. I sent him to the Eighty-third Pennsylvania, nearest to us and better able to take care of him than we were.

TWO FOR EVERY MAN OF US

When we reached the front of the Forty-fourth New York, I thought it far enough. Beyond on the right the Texas Brigade had rallied or rendez-voused, I took thought of that. Most of the fugitives before us, rather than run the gauntlet of our whole brigade, had taken the shelter of the rocks of Great Round Top, on our left, as we now faced. It was hazardous to be so far out, in the very presence of so many baffled but far from beaten veterans of Hood's renowned division. A sudden rush on either flank might not only cut us off, but cut in behind us and seize that vital point which it was our orders and our trust to hold. But it was no light task to get our men to stop.

They were under the momentum of their deed. They thought they were "on the road to Richmond." They had to be reasoned with, per-suaded, but at last faced about and marched back to that dedicated crest with swelling hearts.

Not without sad interest and service was the return. For many of the wounded had to be gathered up. There was a burden, too, of the living. Nearly four hundred prisoners remained in our hands—two for every man of ours.

THE FAREWELL MESSENGERS

Shortly the twilight deepened, and we disposed ourselves to meet any new assault that might come from the courage of exasperation. But the attack was not renewed. Whether that cold steel had chilled the ardor, which flaming muzzles seem to enliven and sustain, or the revulsion of the retiring mood was not yet over, a wide silence brooded over the hostile line. Our worn-out men, bid at last to rest, fitted themselves to their environment or followed their souls' behest. Some bent as if senseless to the earth, some gazed up at the stars and sent wireless messages through them to dear ones far-away; some wandered dreamily away in a search for water to wash from their throats the nitrous fumes of battle; others too manly to seek a surgeon, looked even for a shred of cartridge paper to staunch a too free wound, or yet more deeply drawn sought the sheltered nook where our wounded had been borne to needy such aid as they could, and take the farewell message home from lips of brave men to hearts that had to be more brave.

At nine o'clock the next morning we were withdrawn, being relieved by our First Brigade. But we were sent to anything but a place of rest. Our new position was in support of Hancock's troops near the left center of the Union line, which proved to be the point aimed at by Pickett's charge that afternoon. This is the story of my participation in the action and the passion of the second day at Gettysburg.

It was certainly a narrow chance for us, and for the Round Tops. Had we not used up our ammunition, and had we continued to meet the enemy musket to musket, this "give and take" would soon have finished us by reason of the enemy's superior numbers. Or had the Fifteenth Alabama continued their onset not regarding our preposterous demonstrations, they would have walked over our bodies to their victory. Or, still again, if one more Confederate regiment had come upon our flank, we must have been rolled into a zero figure and swallowed up in the envelopment. It was a psychological success,—a miracle in the scheme of military science. Those brave Alabama fellows—none braver or better in either army—were victims of a surprise, of their quick and mobile imagination.

Return we now to our field and our parting. On the Fourth of July we took part in a reconnaissance over the wreck-strewn field amidst scenes of insupportable horror. Pushing out as far as Willoughby's Run, finding no enemy, we returned to our ground. We were now told to rest and be ready to move from the field the next day.

DEATH'S SOFT WHISPER

But there was neither removal nor rest for us till we had gone up the Round Top slopes to bid farewell to our dead. We found them there on the sheltered lawn where we had laid them, on the velvet moss fringed by the low cedars that veiled the place with peace and beauty. I rode up near, and flinging the rein upon my horse's neck, dismounted to bend over them for a soldier's farewell. There they lay, side by side, with touch of elbow still; brave, bronzed faces where the last thought was written manly resolution, heroic self-giving, divine reconciliation; or where on some fair young face the sweet mother-look, had come out under death's soft whisper.

∿

This passage is clearly the product of a Hearst editor who had never been present on a Civil War battlefield immediately after the fighting ended. Friendly comrades would not have left bodies lying "side by side with touch of elbows still" above the soil. In fact, the 20th Maine was ordered to a new position on Big Round Top soon after the charge, leaving their position, including their little aid station, to reinforcements from the Pennsylvania Reserves. Those men of the 20th Maine who died during or immediately after the fighting on Little Round Top were buried immediately, before their comrades returned from Round Top the following morning. As a result, their graves in the Soldiers National Cemetery are marked as "unknown" since those who buried them had no way to identify their bodies and mark their graves accordingly.

∿

We buried them there, in a grave, alas, too wide, on the sunny side of a great rock, eternal witnesses of their worth—the rock and the sun. Rude head-boards made of ammunition boxes, crudely carved under tear-dimmed eyes, marked and named each grave, and told each home.

I went—it is not long ago—to stand again on that crest whose one day's crown of fire has passed into the blazoned coronet of fame; to look again upon the rocks whereon were laid as on the altar the lives of Vincent and O'Rorke, of Weed and Hazlett—all the chief commanders. And farther on where my own young heroes mounted to fall no more—[Charles W.] Billings, the valor of whose onward-looking eyes not death itself could quench; [Warren L.] Kendall, almost maiden sweet and fair, yet heeding not the bolts that dashed his life-blood on the rocks; Estes and [Sgt. Charles W.] Steele, and Noyes and [Sgt. George W.] Buck, lifted high above self, pure in heart as they that shall see God; and far up the rugged sides of Great Round Top, swept in darkness and silence like its own, were the impetuous [Arad H.] Linscott halted at last before the morning star.

I thought of those other noble men of every type, commanders all, who bore their wounds so bravely—many to meet their end on later fields—and those on whose true hearts further high trusts were to be laid. Nor did I forget those others, whether their names are written on the scrolls of honor and fame, or their dust left on some far field and nameless here—nameless never to me, nor nameless, I trust in God, where they are tonight.

I sat there alone, on the storied crest, till the sun went down as it did before over the misty hills, and the darkness crept up the slopes, till from all earthly sight I was buried as with those before. But oh, what radiant companionship rose around, what steadfast ranks of power, what bearing of heroic souls. Oh, the glory that beamed through those nights and days. Nobody will ever know it here!—I am sorry most of all for that. The proud young valor that rose above the mortal, and then at last was mortal after all; the chivalry of hand and heart that in other days and other lands would have sent their names ringing down in song and story!

UNFORGOTTEN SONS OF GOD

They did not know it themselves—those boys of ours whose remembered faces in every home should be cherished symbols of the true, for life or death—what were their lofty deeds of body, mind, heart, soul, on that tremendous day.

Unknown—but kept! The earth itself shall be its treasurer. It holds something of ours besides graves. These strange influences of material nature, its mountains and seas, its sunset skies and nights of stars, its colors and tones and odors, carry something of the mutual, reciprocal. It is a sympathy. On that other side it is represented to us as suffering. The whole creation travailing in pain together, in earnest expectation, waiting for the adoption—having right, then, to some-thing which is to be its own.

And so these Gettysburg hills which lifted up such splendid valor, and drank in such high heart's blood, shall hold the mighty secret in their bosom till the great day of revelation and recompense, when these heights shall flame again with transfigured light—they, too, have part in that adoption, which is the manifestation of the sons of God!

4

THE CHARGE AT FORT HELL

~

In June of 1864 Chamberlain was in command of a brigade of infantry in the 5th Corps as the Union Army of the Potomac tried to outflank Lee's Confederate Army of Northern Virginia and seize the capitol at Richmond from the south. The two armies confronted one another just south of the City of Petersburg, Virginia, about thirty miles below Richmond. As they gathered opposite one another, the Confederates began to dig in and build defense works while the Union forces probed for vulnerabilities.

Reprinted here is Chamberlain's elaborate account of the events surrounding his near-fatal wounding at Petersburg. This piece was never published in his time, though it may have been written as a third piece after "Through Blood and Fire" and "My Story of Fredericksburg" for one of Hearst's magazines, but never submitted after Chamberlain read how the editors there changed his previous submissions.

~

We made a forced march over the James [River], and to the Petersburg front; but we wasted the whole day, so that we lost the end for which this severe march was inflicted on the men—cheerfully carried through by them out of their loyalty and heartiness. My brigade was a splendid one; given me in consideration of my losing my old, Third Brigade through my misfortune at Rappahannock Station, where after the heat of the assault I had taken a night's bivouac on the bare ground and under an open sky, in a damp, driving snow storm. Returning from Georgetown Seminary Hospital, I found my brigade in command of General [Joseph J.] Bartlett of the Sixth Corps. This First Brigade, however, made up to me the loss. It was composed of five regiments from the old First Corps, remnants of [Gen.] Chapman Biddle's and [Gen.] Roy Stone's Brigades, of [Gen. Abner] Doubleday's old Division, and the splendid new regiment, the 187th Pennsylvania; six regiments as good as ever took arms. Veterans, in fact, the five old regiments, having passed through untold hardships and slaughter at Gettysburg, and in truth, some of them looked upon as somewhat shorn of their honor there as well as of their numbers, by reason of not holding on after all was lost—or perhaps for holding on until one of them lost their colors. At any rate, I found them somewhat disheartened when I took them, after Cold Harbor, and I set to work to restore their spirit, and discipline, and assured them I would recover their prestige in the first battle we went into.

On the night of the 17th they all lay out on the ground before the outer works of Petersburg—2,500 or 3,000 men—waiting for the fierce attack we were expecting to make in the morning on the enemy's defensive works, now well strengthened and manned. I had a strange feeling that evening, a premonition of coming ill. I walked down through the ranks of my silent or sleeping men, drawing a blanket more closely over one, and answering the broken murmurs of another, with apprehension yearning over them, thinking of what was before them, and wishing I could do what no mortal could do for them. Having passed all through the deep spreading ranks, I went to my quarters and dropped into an unaccustomed mood. A shadow seemed to brood over me, dark wings folding as it were [or a pall] and wrapping me in their embrace. Something said; "You will not be here again. This is your last."

I had not the habit of taking a dark view of things; although for twenty-seven days and nights together we had been under fire, more or less, never secure from danger for two hours together. I had a buoyant spirit—not light, and far from making light of things—but resolved and ready for my fate, meaning to face it, and not flinch.

But this night, the premonition became oppressive, unbearable, I went out to speak with some of my most intimate friends who were near. Among others I remember, Captain Twitchell, of the 7th Maine Battery. Then to my own colonels; and finally to General Griffin. I bid them all a cheerful good evening, and went on to turn my greeting into a good bye. Most of them took it as ordinary exchange of courtesies; we had got used to sudden farewells, and fate too sudden for farewells; and I do not think much impression was left on any minds. But when I said to Griffin; "I feel like thanking you, General, for more kindnesses than I can recount tonight. I have appreciated them all; but have had no opportunity to speak to you about them before," he looked up and said, "It seems to me this is a queer time for opportunities to pay compliments. We have other things to think of now. You are worn out. You had better turn in and go to sleep. We shall be awake early enough in the morning." "General, this is my last night with you. You must let me thank you. I wish you to know my love for you." "What do you mean," he sharply ejaculates—unwilling perhaps to let me see that he was moved. "I shall fall tomorrow, General; this is my good bye:" "Why do you think so?" he asks. "The dark angel has said it to me." "You have lost your poise. These terrible strains have been too much for you." "No. General; I have perfect balance. You will see that. You will not be ashamed of me."

"My God," he cries, "you are all wrong. I will tell you now what I was not going to. Warren and I have [been] talking things over. It is decided. You have done your full share of fighting. You are not to be put in tomorrow. You are held in reserve. So there." "Yes, General; the reserve goes in when all is lost or must be saved by sacrifice. Let me lead tomorrow." "Drop this; put away this feeling; we can't spare you, and I will not let you be exposed tomorrow." "It will not be for you to say, General; Fate will cast the lot, or has cast it already." "Oh, go to sleep; we will talk about this in the morning, if there is anything to talk about." "Then, Good Night, General."

Morning came with artillery at close range. The enemy knew we were of course preparing to attack their lines, and were using strong disuasives. All was astir in both lines,—Restless, feverish, (it seemed to me knowing only my own front),—unplanned, tentative, or resting on contingencies. Soon our batteries were advanced to reply to those annoying us. The fire came back upon them fiercely. The enemy seemed now contemplating an attempt to take our guns by a dash. Then General Griffin rode up and said, "We wish you would look out for these batteries here. They may try to take them." "Certainly, General; they shall not take them," was the quiet assurance. He then rode away. I moved up close in rear of the guns, covering my men as I could by taking advantage of the ground. But the cannonading was sharp; the shot and shell tore up the whole ground in front of us. I had to ride along up & down the front of my men to reassure them; for many were falling, with no chance to strike back; and this is hard to bear. I knew that something different must be done, and soon; and was rather nervous myself. Then Griffin and Warren rode up to me; Griffin spoke: "It is too bad: I tried to prevent this; but those batteries out there must be dislodged. General Warren asks if you will do it." "Does General Warren order this?" I asked. "I have a thought about it, and wish to know what the orders are." "We do not order it; we wish it, if it is possible to be done. But it is a hard push up that open slope." "That was what I was planning about, General; Will you let me do it in my own way? I think I can clear the batteries away—perhaps take them." "Well, I am sorry for this; you will not think hard of me in any way?" "I am thinking hard, but not of you," was the word as I rode up to my senior colonel and gave him orders to take the brigade to the left, not towards the enemy, but on parallel line somewhat sheltered from the enemy's fire, and mostly from their sight. I directed him to gain a piece of woods on the right flank of the enemy's guns and wait for me. Then I turned and gave rein to my horse, and headed straight for the rebel batteries. I had seen something which looked not quite right, between us and the batteries; something I could not understand, looking, however, like a line of rifle pits for infantry, in front of their guns. I wished to see what this was, and there was no other way. I was not going to push my brave men up to it, and possibly have them annihilated there. I was riding, of course, at headlong speed. Soon I was aware of a tearing Tartar overtaking me, and rushing up to my side. "What in the name of Heaven are you going to do?" cries Griffin. "I am just going to look at that strange ground there," was the reply, without checking speed. "Then I am going with you," shouts Griffin.

Meanwhile the Rebels seeing the strange embassy had begun to burst shell right over our heads and almost in our faces. We were aware that people from both armies were looking on, astonished, not knowing what circus-riding this was.

"There, you see, General, what I feared. I was not going to put my men up here." It was a deep railroad cut, and earth thrown up high as a man's breast just below the range of the enemy's artillery. Their shot would skim the crest and mow men down like reaping-machines. We both wheeled like a flash, with a half smile, strangely significant; he to his place with the center of his other brigades—I to my clump of woods, first taking a line to the rear before bearing to my [division's] left where my brigade was crossing the railroad track at level grade.

We followed a rough track up to the woods, and there formed in two lines, with two regiments as a flanking force to support me on the left. I then instructed all the field officers what my plans were. We were to advance noiselessly as possible through the woods, and [on] emerging, fire there a volley & make a rush upon the flank of the rebel guns, and overwhelm them if possible before they could recover their wits. The second line was to follow the first at a distance of 100 yards, till their line came to join with the first or replace it. It was a situation where the commander should lead; for quick action and change of action would be required. So

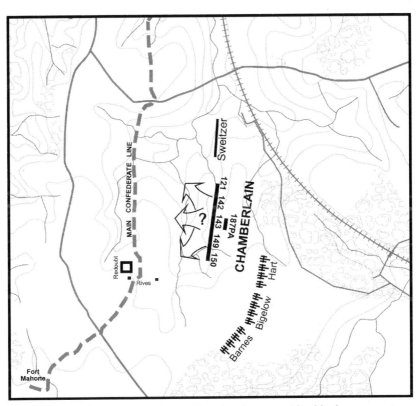

Chamberlain's Charge at Petersburg—There has been considerable disagreement and debate as to the exact line of attack taken by Chamberlain and his brigade on June 18 and thus the location of his near-fatal wound. The location is shown here but we will likely never know the exact angle and direction that he and his men took.

with the whole staff, flag flying aloft, and the splendid lines close pressing, we made for the guns.

Then a burst of artillery fire turned upon us with terrible effect. Down went my horse under me, a piece of case shot going through him; down went every one of my staff wounded or unhorsed; down went my red Maltese cross, flag of our brigade; but on went everybody, on for the guns. Enfilading fire from great guns on our left, tore the earth before us, behind us, around us, through us; the batteries swung and gave us canister, & before we could reach them, limbered up and got off down the slope under cover of their main entrenchments. We only got their ground, and drove away the guns. I was mortified, greatly troubled. But the enfilading fire was so heavy we had to get a little below the crest we had carried, and prepare to hold it against attempts to recover it. Pondering and studying the situation, I saw that we could use artillery to advantage. I sent back to Griffin or Warren, a mile, I should think for some artillery, meanwhile setting my pioneers to digging platforms just under the crest of the hill, making level ground for the guns to be worked on when they should arrive. Before long, up came [Capt. John] Bigelow with the 9th Massachusetts, and [Capt. Patrick] Hart of the 15th New York, followed by another, [Capt. Almont] Barnes' 1st New York. [Capt. Charles E.] Mink was across the cut firing in the Ice House to my right front. We helped the guns up into the places I had made for them, laying their muzzles in the grass close to the earth, so that nobody could suspect we had artillery there. We were so far advanced from the rest of the army that I did not quite like to give the enemy a chance to study up plans to capture our exposed guns; but I put two good regiments, the 150th, and [left blank] regiments, to guard the exposed left flank, and busied myself in strengthening our position.

∾

Chamberlain was unaware, but by his forward movement and driving the enemy artillery, he had drawn considerable attention to himself in the midst of a growingly volatile situation among the senior leaders of the army. For the entire campaign to date, General Grant, commander of all of the Union armies in the field, had chosen to remain physically with the Army of the Potomac. This placed Gen. George G. Meade, who had been in command of this army since three days before Gettysburg nearly a year earlier, in the unenviable situation of commanding an army with his boss seldom more than a mile away, sometimes telling him how he should act, sometimes ordering his subordinates to act in ways Meade may not have wished. With the potential for the end of the war hanging in the balance, and perhaps on whether the enemy could throw up impenetrable works before he could attack them in force, the stakes were high and immediate.

Meade's reputation for losing his violent temper was legendary in the army, and he was even more ornery than usual this day. As an aide later remembered, "The General was in a tearing humor."* His disposition did not improve upon the arrival of a dispatch he had just received from General Warren, Chamberlain's corps commander. In it, Warren notified Meade, his commander, that he had not attacked the rebel lines an hour earlier as ordered, but instead had other advice for the general in charge. "I think," Warren dared suggest, "it would be safe for us all to make a rush at, say, 3 p.m." General Ambrose Burnside commanded the corps adjacent to Warren, and Meade had also ordered him to launch an attack which he had failed to do. To the dispatch now reaching Meade, he had added, "I fully concur in the statement of General Warren."†

Meade's reply to this near mutiny was unusually blunt and left no doubt that he had reached the end of his famously limited patience. Soon after, a scathing dispatch was en route to both corps commanders, Major-Generals Warren and Burnside:

> I am greatly astonished at your dispatch of 2 p.m. What additional orders to attack you require I cannot imagine. My orders have been explicit and are now repeated, that you each immediately assault the enemy with all your force, and if there is any further delay the responsibility and the consequences will rest with you.
>
> Geo. G. Meade, Major-General.‡

Desperate for action from anyone in command of anything in his army, Meade saw what he needed in Chamberlain's successful assault on the enemy artillery and he acted without delay. The exchange with the staff officer and the reply that resulted, however, were not the kind to brighten Meade's mood.

In the midst of this, a staff-officer came out, much excited with his difficult journey, and gave me the order: "The General commanding, (he did not say which general, it was either Meade or Grant; it was not an officer I had seen before), desires you to attack and carry the works in your front."

---

* Meade's *Headquarters, 1863–1865: Letters of Colonel Theodore Lyman from the Wilderness to Appomattox.* Atlantic Monthly Press, 1922, pp. 168–69.

† *Official Records*, Series 1, Vol. 40, pt. 2 p. 179.

‡ *Official Records*, Series 1, Vol. 40, pt. 2 p. 179.

"Does the General know where I am?" I asked. "Let me show you! They are the interior works, the main works at Petersburg, and am I to attack alone?" "I gave you the order," he says, "that is all I have to say." "Very well, Colonel, you are Colonel ############# are you not?" "I am sir." "Will you kindly take a written message from me to the General?" "Certainly, if you wish; I see that there may be occasion for it." "There is," I said.

And I took out my field-book and wrote as follows:

"I have received the order to assault the enemy's main works in my front. The General commanding cannot possibly be aware of the situation here. From where I write this I can count ten or twelve pieces of artillery behind earthworks, so placed as to give me a cross-fire, and a line of works with not less than 5,000 infantry, easily sweeping the slope down which I must advance not less than 300 yards from this point. A large Fort is on my left and perfectly enfilades with heavy guns the whole slope in my front. It will be only slaughter for men to charge upon this front, unsupported. Fully aware of the responsibility I assume, my duty to my veteran soldiers compels me to ask to postpone this charge until the General can be informed of the circumstances. In my opinion, if an assault is to be made, it should be by not less than the whole Army of the Potomac."

I thought it likely that it was not known at head quarters that I had carried this crest. The order might have meant this "crest." No sooner had this hasty message left my control than I began to reflect on the presumptuous character of giving my unasked opinion about the assault. I was not commanding the Army of the Potomac, and my last remark was uncalled for and highly censurable. Whatever might be said of an officer, in any manner refusing to attack the enemy when ordered to do so, this pert advice about the Army of the Potomac being the only proper agent of an assault was unpardonable. How I could have been such a fool, passed my understanding, + [I began to think] my premonition about this being my last day in the field would soon be realized. I expected nothing less than an "arrest" and an order to the rear for charges of the most serious kind known to the service. I began to think what influence I could bring bear upon the President, through [U.S. Senator William] Pitt Fessenden, [Congressman] Henry Wilson, [U.S. Senator] Charles Sumner [both of Massachusetts], and [Maine Congressman] Lot Morrill, to secure a pardon before sentence. I called my Colonels up and told them I expected soon to be taken away. I did not tell them how. I gave them however my general ideas of the situation, and of the best manner of making an assault when ordered. It is needless to say that I was in a very distressed state of mind,—shame above all, taking the "pith" all out of me. In about half an hour I saw the same staff-officer coming up the rear slope of the crest. I was ready to give up my sword. I was a pitiful thing,—I worn thin, burnt brown, taxed and tasked beyond my powers by severe service. I had unflinchingly and uncomplainingly rendered, and having just achieved a good piece of work for which I knew I deserved praise,—to be seen disarmed, disgraced, sneaking to the rear, with not even the dignity of a lamb led to the slaughter, but more like a dog kicked away from decent company. (It never occurred to me,—not having the opportunity to secure counsel, to plead insanity.)

In this lowest pit of dejection, the staff-officer approached. "Yes, Sir, I am ready," was my first word, spoken before he came to a stand. "The General says you are quite right in what you say about the assault. The whole army will attack." I felt as if I were on wings. Life, death, had no "terrors." "But," and here came in the balancer, the "twist" pretty fairly getting even with me for my pertness, "from the position of things, you being advanced as you are, it will be necessary to guide on you. You will be the "battalion of direction." The General wishes to know the precise minute when you will be ready to attack."

"Now!" I greedily answered, glad to gulp down any medicine, as a punishment for that sin of foolishness, for which no provision seems to be made in the [economies] of nature or grace. "Oh, no," he responds, "that will not give time to get the order to all the commands. But we want an hour fixed, for simult[ane]ous movement." "Very well, sir, how much time will it take?" "Perhaps an hour," he replies. I took out my watch, and compared it with his; "I will attack at 3 o'clock, precisely" was my final word.

No more dejection now. It was projection. And lively at that. The artillery had meanwhile been getting up and into the platforms I had partly prepared. This suited me well. The muzzles would be laid right in the short grass on the crest when pushed into action, but were protected when loading after the recoil. I went along the rear of the guns advising with the commanding officer about getting a slant fire on the enemy's guns in the works before and slightly below us, so as to knock them off of their trunnions if possible, and be ready to give case shot or canister when demonstration of the enemy should offer good effects. My chief solicitude was lest this fire which I directed to open only when my men were well down in front below the line of their fire, should demoralize or injure my men, by the stripping lead of the band of shell or too premature bursting of case shot above their heads. I also gave particular instruction to my colonels, especially to the two senior colonels likely to succeed me. I did not conceal from them my expectation of not long surviving; for I resolved to lead the charge in person.

I held my watch in hand, and when the minute hand was on the mark for 3 o'clock, I told the bugler to sound the "charge."

Up rose my brave men; past the batteries they press; closing in in front of them; down the slope they go; muskets on the shoulder; bayonets fixed; for I had instructed on no account to commence firing in front of the enemy's works, this would distract their attention from the main purpose, which was to go over the works, and taking them any way hand to hand. As I had determined, I led the movement with my whole staff, dismounted,—the horses had all gone down under the fierce fire we encountered in carrying the crest at first. I had a color-bearer following me, also on foot.

At this outburst of men after a moment's astonishment, the enemy opened with every kind of missile man has invented. My men being below the line of fire of our own artillery, this began too, with whatever it could best use,—solid shot, first, shell short-fused—the distance was from 200 yards to 400 according to objects needing engagement,—and what I dreaded, case-shot,—from which some explosions troubled my men,—or possibly, the stripping lead and sabots. Now rose such a fury of fire as never was concentrated on one small space before; crowned by the heavy fire of Fort Mahone on our left, which as soon as we got fairly in front of our own guns had perfect enfilading range, & used it "well"—in their estimation no doubt. I had formed two lines three regiments in the front line and the 187th in the second, a "new" regiment, full ranks, and stout hearts; with two regiments skilled marksmen as a special column on the left to guard that exposed flank in whatever way should be necessary. This now seems to me not the best formation; for it gave my new regiment the awful spectacle of the havoc made in my first line; my reason for this was, however, that none but experienced soldiers should try to go over works with the bayonet. And the two gallant regiments I had placed in column, (they were small in numbers) on the left, were a good,—bad,—mark for all the demons that had at their mercy, front and flank. But I had thought it necessary to guard strongly that unsupported flank, especially as an attempt would be made I thought it likely, to capture my artillery, which had no chance to get out except right in the face of some batteries now disclosed on my left. A very exposed, and dangerous position for them, unless strongly supported, which I saw, from my advanced ground when clear of the crest, had utterly failed to make effective demonstration. I cannot say there was any "surprise" anywhere; I had perfectly comprehended all that happened, before I moved a step, and had so told the staff-officer bringing me the orders. For some reason I do not now feel able to state I had no confidence that the expected "support" promised me would amount to any thing. It proved true; that was all. So I do not know that I was at fault in my dispositions, however severely they exposed my command. My main business was to take the works in front. What kind of a situation we should be in then, with Mahone pouring its great shot down on us, unless the miracle should be wrought of our other troops carrying or silencing it, I hardly charged myself with thinking; that was for my superiors, "commanding the Army of the Potomac."

In five minutes' time my flag-bearer was shot dead. I took the flag from his dying hands, without a look at the poor fellow, and pressed on. My staff were being disabled—some with wounds, some sent to watch or help the various points of greatest danger, especially my left. The very earth was plowed and torn to pieces by the shot directed at my troops, a clear mark on the side hill for the whole force of the enemy from every quarter. The great shot from the fort on the left sent the turf and stones through our ranks, filling the air with tornado debris. The musketry was like a boiling sea. Suddenly I found myself on the borders of a marsh or bog, which men could not well pass. This must not catch my men, I thought, and made a half face to the left and gave the command, "Incline to the left. To the left." Nobody could hear a word—any more than at the bottom of Hell. I raised the flag, the red cross, high as I could and waving this in one hand and my saber with the other towards the left, continued shouting and signaling, "To the left. To the left." In the hiss and roar and blinding, flying earth, standing and so signaling I felt a sharp hot flush that seemed to cut the spinal marrow out of my back-bone. A twelve-pound shell or case-shot had exploded right behind me as I was faced, and the pieces came thrumming by my ears. My thought was that I had been shot in the back—in the middle of the back, below the belt. This was all I could think of for a moment, and the shame of it was worse than death. To be shot in the back, in the face of the enemy! This was worse than refusing to attack. I was lost, dead or alive, and better dead! I had not fallen. That was strange for the blow was strong. But I was well braced as I stood waving my two emblems of command; and braced also in mind, had not fallen. Perforce I dropped flag-staff and saber to the ground; holding them upright, however, without claiming much heroism for that, as I had need of both for my staff and stand. But I put on an extreme straightness of posture, wishing to countervail the appearance of cowardly turning my back to the enemy and getting proof of it in the telling shot. It never occurred to me that an officer leading his men in a charge might properly have to face aside to give effect to a command. I remember and always shall, the looks on the faces of my men as they came up to me in line,—dear, brave fellows—their writhing line stiff and strong as the links of a chain-cable, as they broke files [and] gave way to the left—to pass obstacle. I glanced. I could see the sorry but half-forgiving look as they thought I was showing the white feather,—letting them pass me to the terrible front of which come even now bellowings and bursts spitting lead and hurtling iron. A minute has not passed, when as I turned to look sharply at my second line, my noble new regiment coming up so grandly into this terrible test, I felt in my sword hand a gush of hot blood.

I looked down then for the first time. I saw the blood spurting out of my right hip-side, and saw that it had already filled my long cavalry boots to overflowing, and also my baggy reinforced trousers, and was running out at both pocket welts. Not shot in the back then! I do not think I was ever so happy in my life. My first thought was of my Mother, my Huguenot-blooded mother; how glad she would be that her boy was not shot in the back!

"Had he his wounds before?" Then it is well. I found that I had been shot through by a minie ball—the round hole was plain,—from hip joint to hip joint,—from right to left, just in front of the joints. I was already faint with loss of blood. I sank first to my knees, then leaning on my right elbow. One of my staff ran up now—Major Funk—and fell distracted with grief on my very body, begging me to let him go for a surgeon, or have me taken to one. I knew either to be impossible, and useless. "No" I said, "my dear fellow; there is much better for you to do on this field. I saw movement from the enemy's lines just as I was struck, to take the batteries on the crest. Run to the 150th Pennsylvania and tell them to take care of those guns at all events, and tell Bigelow or Hart to prepare to give canister in his front, but look for our men and not fire into them. We will take care of his left flank." Then came up Major Osborne Jones, inspector on my staff—agonized. "Tell Colonel [Irvin] that he is in command of the brigade," I said. "The assault is checked; I can see that. Get the men where they will not be destroyed. Don't let them try to stand here under this fire. Either over, or out!" I would not let him try to get me away. It would not be worth the cost. I could see that my assault had failed and that a countercharge was preparing men; were already coming over their works beyond our left, and forming for attack. This must be attended to. That was my chief thought. I lay now straight out on my back, too weak to move a limb; the blood forming a pool, under and around me—more blood than the books allow a man. I had not much pain. It was more a stunning blow, a kind of dull tension, my teeth shut sharp together hard, like lock-jaw. So I lay looking, thinking, sinking, the tornado tearing over and around. Dull hoarse faint cries in the low air: hisses, spatters, thuds, thunderbolts mingling earth and sky, and I moistening the little space of mother-earth for a cabbage garden for some poor fellow, black or white, unthinking, unknowing. I had lain here an hour, perhaps, when I was aware of some men standing over me, with low-toned voices debating with themselves what to do. I spoke to them. They brightened up, and said they were sent to bring me off the field. I told them it was of no good; I was not worth it, emphasizing this in such terms that they replied that they had positive orders. I told them I would give orders for them to go back. "Begging pardon," they said "but you are not in command now." This rather roused me, which only seemed to prove to them that I was worth saving. I told them they could not get up that slope without getting killed, every one of them. But they took me up, put me on their stretcher, and started. Not 20 yards away when came one of those great shots from the Fort on the left striking in the very spot from which they had lifted me, and digging a grave there large enough for all us, scattering the earth and gravel all over us, with rather unpleasant force. The next minute a musket ball broke an arm for one of my carriers. Another took his place, and they steered for the right of the batteries, around which they managed to pass and set me down behind the batteries, below the range of shot skimming overhead. Captain Bigelow gave me all the attention possible, which was more relief to him than practical avail to me, a limp mass of bloody earth. After a while an ambulance came galloping up to the foot of the hill, and I was put into it, and galloped through rough stumpy fields to a cluster of pines where our Division had a rude field hospital. Most of the surgeons there had been or were attached to my headquarters, and I knew and loved them, for they were noble men. The first thing done was to lay me upon a table improvised from a barn-window or door, and examine the wound. I remember somebody taking a ram rod of a musket and running it through my body—it was too wide for any surgeon's probe—to discover the bullet, which they did not at first observe sticking up with a puff of skin just behind my left hip joint. This they soon cut out, and closed the cut with a bandage not knowing what might need to be done with this opening. Some slight dressing was put upon the round hole on the right side, and I was gently laid on a pile of pine boughs gathered by some kindly, and perhaps sorrowing hands. Around me were several badly wounded officers both of our army and of the Confederate. On my right, his feet touching mine, noble Colonel Prescott of the 32 Massachusetts, with a bullet in his breast; on the other side, a fine-faced, young Confederate officer, badly wounded and suffering terribly. The whole little space was strewn thick with such cases as these. It was not cheerful. Soon, just as the shadows grew thick, a group of surgeons stood not far off earnestly discussing something, looking at me now and then. I knew what it was. One of them said to another; "You do it." "No. I can't" was the reply. But I beckoned one of them to me and said, "I know what troubles you. I know all about it. You have done your best. It is a mortal wound. I know this, and am prepared for it. I have been for a long time." "Yes, there is no possible chance for you. We could not tell you. You can not live till morning." "So be it, you can't help me. But you can save poor Prescott; look to him. We won't leave you, Prescott," I turned to say—with voice rather feeble for such stout proffer of aid. And here is this poor fellow, this rebel officer, suffering much. Help him all you can. He is far from home. He is ours now."

I had got a leaf from a field order book and written with a pencil a brief letter to my young wife; telling her how it was; bidding her and our two little ones to God's keeping, and folded my hands with nothing more for them to do.

It was a lurid, wild, cloud-driven sunset—like my own. Griffin came over to me with Bartlett and I think Warren and some of the Corps staff. Griffin did not know what to say. Indeed there was nothing to say, of the future, or of the present—and what avail now, of the past? I think I spoke first, and it may seem strange in such circumstances that I should begin almost playfully;—Well, General, you see I was right. Here I am, at the end. And here you are, as I knew you would be. But it is time to report. I have carried the crest." "You are going to pull through" he says. In spite of them all, you will pull through. It will come out all right," he says. "Yes, but I would have had some things otherwise," I answered.

"Do you know," he eagerly returns, "Grant has promoted you! He has sent his word! He will write an order about it." "Has he? That will not help me now. But it will do good. I thank the General."

"I thank you, and all of you for this kindness." They did not know how narrowly I had escaped cashiering, as I did. They spoke of my promotion and the manner of it. They all spoke gentle words, some praisingly. But Griffin came up near, took my hand and said: "Now keep a stiff upper lip. We will stand by you. Meade knows about it. It will be all right." "Yes, General."— "Good Night."—"Good Night." But I saw in the glimmering twilight his hand drawn across his eyes and his shoulder shiver and heave quite visibly, even to my fading eyes. Then I folded my hands again across my chest.

After a while of this stupor suddenly came a flood of tearing agony. I never dreamed what pain could be and not kill a man outright. My pity went back to men I had seen helpless on the stricken field. The pain wore into a stupor. Then through the mists I looked up and saw dear, faithful Doctor Shaw, Surgeon of my own regiment [the 20th Maine] lying a mile away. My brother Tom had brought him. He and good Dr. Townsend sat down by me and tried to use some instrument to establish proper connection to stop the terrible extravasations which would end my life. All others had given it up, and me too. But these two faithful men bent over their task trying with vain effort to find the entrance to torn and clogged and distorted passages of vital currents. Toiling and returning to the ever impossible task, the able surgeon undertaking to aid Dr. Shaw said, sadly, "It is of no use, Doctor; he cannot be saved. I have done all possible for man. Let us go, and not torture him longer." "Just once more, Doctor; let me try just this once more, and I will give it up." Bending to his task, by a sudden miracle, he touched the exact lost thread; the thing was done. There was a possibility, only that even now, that I might be there to know in the morning. Tom stood over me like a brother, and such a one as he was. True-hearted [Col. Ellis] Spear [then commanding the 20th Maine] with him, watching there like guardians over a cradle amidst the wolves of the wilderness.

After midnight I became aware of some one fumbling about my beard, trying to find my mouth amidst the ragged mass of beard. The great iron spoon made its way along the uncertain track made by his trembling hand. I opened my eyes and there knelt Spear, his red beard in the gleam of a lurid campfire making him look like a picture of one of the old masters. He had been turning the spoon bowl as he thought in the right place, but had missed it by an inch, and the beverage he was offering had taken the course nearest to the earth, which was down my neck and bosom outside. "Now, please give me some," I plaintively murmured, taking a little cheer, if I can be believed, in making a joke of it. The tears were running down his cheeks, and I thought, into the black tin dipper; but he smiled through them—and taken all together, it was a good porridge. At times the agonizing pains would get the better of my patience. But sufferings of those lying around me, particularly of the poor forlorn southerner close to me, were some counterpoise. "A fellow feeling makes us wondrous kind." At dawn dear brave Prescott was dead, and I alive. Griffin had been stirring. Meade had sent a stretcher and 8 men to carry me 16 miles to City Point, to be taken by steamer to Annapolis. That was thought the only way to save me. If I could be got into a tent by the seashore, with skillful treatment, and favorable surroundings, it was thought, it seems that there might be a chance for me. Friends gathered to see my "forlorn hope" move out. It was a blazing day. My bearers were none too many. I felt Meade's kind thoughtfulness which I had no particular reason to expect. This was probably Griffin's doing, although the order for the detail came from Meade. The great loss of blood had weakened me to the extreme. The men tried to screen my face from the burning sun, and to relieve my faintness by moistened cl[oths] laid over it. But it was a hard day for them—this 16 miles march with this wearying load. I wish I could have had the names of those men so as to follow them in life.

At City Point I was transferred to a steamer—my stretcher set down on the main deck. I was told there were 600 badly wounded officers on board. There was something in the air which testified this, both to the senses and to the mysterious "inner sense." I felt the whole, as well as my part, of the mournful embassy. The thought, too, of the "government" taking care of us stricken, broken bodies, was grateful. But the journey was long, and the night and morning dreary. The surgeon in charge had braced himself for his task a little too much, and came near going over backwards. We—the people on my deck suffered for lack of proper care. We were in wretched condition broken, maimed, torn, stiffened with clotted blood and matted hair and beard, dazed with that strange sensation of being suddenly cut down from the full flush of vigorous health to hardly breathing bodies.

We did not know what we wanted—nor did anybody else, apparently. But by some fortunate accident Dr. Tom Moses, one of my old College boys who had charge of the upper deck, learned that I was below, and he lost no time in coming to my side; and he was virtually there all that dismal night.

It seemed to me some time after the second midnight that I was set on the wharf at Annapolis Naval School, and left there a long time before my turn came, and then it was to be taken into a naked dreary tent. There I lay entirely alone for hours. The first disturbance I had was seeing the flap of my tent open and a kindly, earnest face looking in, and then the whole form of woman's divineness came to me, with the question, "Who are you?" If she had said "What are you," it would have been justified. A more uncanny looking being, I suppose, never stood across a human pathway.

"Booted and spurred," blood-soaked and smeared, hair and beard matted with blood and earth, where I had lain on the earth amidst the flying turf and stones, pale as death and weak as water—I was a poor witness of what I was, or who. But from that moment no tenderness that man or angel could show was left unfulfilled by this Boston girl, Mary Clark. She interested Dr. Vanderkieft in my case, & he sent Welsh "Tommy" to serve me, and I had all the surgical skill that the French army or the United States could command, and all the care that divine womanhood could divine. But it was a "far cry to Lochow." For two months wrestling at the gates of death, in agonies inexpressible, though direfully enough betokened, convulsions, death-chills, lashings, despairing surgeons, waiting embalmers— "rejected addresses"—and all this under the eyes of the dear, suffering wife, who had taken up her dwelling in the adjoining tent. Through this valley of the shadow of death—in five months back at the front with my men!

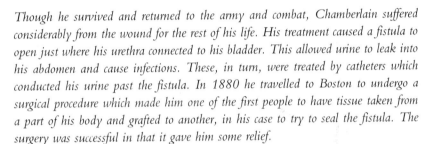

Though he survived and returned to the army and combat, Chamberlain suffered considerably from the wound for the rest of his life. His treatment caused a fistula to open just where his urethra connected to his bladder. This allowed urine to leak into his abdomen and cause infections. These, in turn, were treated by catheters which conducted his urine past the fistula. In 1880 he travelled to Boston to undergo a surgical procedure which made him one of the first people to have tissue taken from a part of his body and grafted to another, in his case to try to seal the fistula. The surgery was successful in that it gave him some relief.

A few months short of the fiftieth anniversary of this wound, Chamberlain passed away in his home in Portland, Maine. Dr. Abner Shaw, who had saved his life at Petersburg and treated him ever since, was by his side. Whether as a medical fact, or as some sympathetic gesture, Dr. Shaw listed the Petersburg wound as part of the cause of his death, making him, symbolically and on paper, at least, the last Civil War soldier to die of his wounds.

5

APPOMATTOX

∾

"Paper Read before the New York Commandery Loyal Legion of the United States October Seventh, 1903 by General Joshua L. Chamberlain." The Military Order of the Loyal Legion of the United States (MOLLUS) was an organization made up of former Union Army officers who, on occasion, would sponsor lectures by their comrades describing their personal memories of significant events during the war. Each state had a "Commandery" that published these lectures in book form. During the postwar years, Chamberlain spoke to these groups in several states.

Among these lectures was perhaps his most comprehensive reminiscence of the surrender at Appomattox, excepting perhaps the section of his book The Passing of the Armies *that deals with the surrender.*

Chamberlain's observations are significant because he was the highest-ranking officer at the point where Confederate infantry units, at the insistence of General Grant in the terms of surrender, were to march up and stack their arms and flags in a formal and symbolic act of submission. Grant required this before they could receive their parole, a pass giving them the legal freedom to move across the countryside to return to their homes. In this role, Chamberlain effectively commanded the moment of surrender of each regiment of General Robert E. Lee's Army of Northern Virginia. In the course of this narrative, Chamberlain also reveals that he was the first general officer among the Union forces to receive word from the official Confederate messenger of Lee's desire to surrender his army.

∾

I am to speak of what came under my observation in the action at Appomattox Courthouse and the circumstances attending the surrender of the Army of Northern Virginia, April 9, 1865.

You will understand that I am not attempting to present matters upon a uniform scale or to mark the relative merits of participants. This is only the story of what I saw and felt and thought,—in fact, my personal experience, including something of the emotions awakened and the reflections suggested by that momentous consummation.

In order that you may understand the pressure of conditions and the temper of our spirits in this last action, permit me to recur briefly to the situation of affairs. The great blow had been struck, the long hold loosened. Lee's communications had been cut; his intrenched lines broken and overrun; his right rolled up; Richmond and Petersburg evacuated by the Confederate forces and officials, and in our possession; his broken army in full retreat, or rather, desperately endeavoring to get off,—either to Danville, to effect a junction with [Gen. Joseph E.] Johnston in North Carolina, or to Lynchburg, where they might rally for one more forlorn but possibly long resistance. Meade with two corps of the Army of the Potomac—the Second and Sixth—was pressing Lee's rear; while [Gen. Phillip] Sheridan with his cavalry—three divisions—and our Fifth Corps of infantry under [Gen. Charles] Griffin was making a flying march to circumvent Lee's path and plans; our combined forces all the while seeking to draw him to final battle, or compel him to surrender.

The 8th of April found the Fifth Corps at Prospect Station, on the South Side Railroad, nearly abreast of the head of Lee's retreating column, while Meade was with his two corps close upon Lee's rear at New Store, ten miles north of us, across the Appomattox. At noon of this day General [Edward O. C.] Ord, of the Army of the James, joined us with two divisions of the Twenty-fourth Corps under General [John] Gibbon, and [David B.] Birney's division of the Twenty-fifth Corps,—colored troops; Ord, by virtue of seniority, becoming commanding officer of the whole. He was a stranger to us all, but his simple and cordial manner towards Sheridan and Griffin, and even to us subordinates, made him welcome. We pushed on,—the cavalry ahead.

The Fifth Corps had a very hard march that day, made more so in the afternoon and night by the lumbering obstructions of the rear of Ord's tired column, by courtesy given the road before us, the incessant check fretting our men almost to mutiny. We had been rushed all day to keep up with the cavalry, but this constant checking was worse. We did not know that Grant had sent orders for the Fifth Corps to march all night without halting; but it was not necessary for us to know it. After twenty-nine miles of this kind of marching, at the blackest hour of night, human nature called a halt. Dropping by the roadside, right and left, wet or dry, down went the men as in a swoon. Officers slid out of saddle, loosened the girth, slipped an arm through a loop of bridle-rein, and sunk to sleep. Horses stood with drooping heads just above their masters' faces. All dreaming,—one knows not what, of past or coming, possible or fated.

Scarcely is the first broken dream begun when a cavalry man comes splashing down the road, and vigorously dismounts, pulling from his jacket front a crumpled note. The sentinel standing watch by his commander, worn in body but alert in every sense, touches your shoulder. "Orders, sir, I think!" You rise on elbow, strike a match, and with smarting, streaming eyes read the brief, thrilling note, from Sheridan—like this, as I remember: "I have cut across the enemy at Appomattox Station, and captured three of his trains. If you can possibly push your infantry up here to-night, we will have great results in the morning." Ah, sleep no more! The startling bugle notes ring out "The General"—"To the march!" Word is sent for the men to take a bite of such as they had for food: the promised rations would not be up till noon, and by that time we should be—where? Few try to eat, no matter what.

Meanwhile, almost with one foot in the stirrup you take from the hands of the black boy* a tin plate of nondescript food and a dipper of miscalled coffee,—all equally black, like the night around. You eat and drink at a swallow; mount, and away to get to the head of the column before you sound the "Forward." They are there—the men: shivering to their senses as if risen out of the earth, but something in them not of it Now sounds the "Forward," for the last time in our long-drawn strife; and they move— these men—sleepless, supperless, breakfastless, sore-footed, stiff-jointed, sense-benumbed, but with flushed faces pressing for the front.

By sunrise we have reached Appomattox Station, where Sheridan has left the captured trains. A staff-officer is here to turn us square to the right,—to the Appomattox River, cutting across Lee's retreat. Already we hear the sharp ring of the horse-artillery, answered ever and anon by heavier field guns; and drawing nearer, the crack of cavalry carbines; and unmistakeably, too, the graver roll of musketry of infantry. There is no mistake. Sheridan is square across the enemy's front, and with that glorious cavalry alone is holding at bay all that is left of the proudest army of

---

* Army regulations provided general officers with an additional allowance to hire a servant. The "black boy" was Chamberlain's.

the Confederacy. It has come at last,—the supreme hour! No thought of human wants or weakness now: all for the front; all for the flag, for the final stroke to make its meaning real. These men of the Potomac and the James, side by side, at the double in time and column, now one and now the other in the road or the fields beside. One striking feature I can never forget,—Birney's black men abreast with us, pressing forward to save the white man's country.

I had two brigades, my own and [Gen. Edgar] Gregory's, about midway of our hurrying column. Upon our intense procession comes dashing out of a woods road on the right a cavalry staff-officer. With sharp salutation he exclaims: "General Sheridan wishes you to break off from this column and come to his support. The rebel infantry is pressing him hard. Our men are falling back. Don't wait for orders through the regular channels, but act on this at once!"

Sharp work now! Guided by the staff-officer, at cavalry speed we break out from the column and push through the woods, right upon Sheridan's battle-flag gleaming amidst the smoke of his batteries in the edge of the open field. Weird-looking flag it was: fork-tailed, red and white, the two bands that composed it each charged with a star of the contrasting color; two eyes sternly glaring through the cannon-cloud. Beneath it, that storm-centre spirit, that form of condensed energies, mounted on the grim charger, Rienzi, that turned the battle of the Shenandoah,—both, rider and steed, of an unearthly shade of darkness, terrible to look upon, as if masking some unknown powers.

Right before us, our cavalry, Devins's division, gallantly stemming the surges of the old Stonewall brigade, desperate to beat its way through. I ride straight to Sheridan. A dark smile and impetuous gesture are my only orders. Forward into double lines of battle, past Sheridan, his guns, his cavalry, and on for the quivering crest! For a moment it is a glorious sight: every arm of the service in full play,—cavalry, artillery, infantry; then a sudden shifting scene as the cavalry, disengaged by successive squadrons, rally under their bugle-calls with beautiful precision and promptitude, and sweep like a storm-cloud beyond our right to close in on the enemy's left and complete the fateful envelopment.

We take up the battle. Gregory follows in on my left. It is a formidable front we make. The scene darkens. In a few minutes the tide is turned; the incoming wave is at high flood; the barrier recedes. In truth, the Stonewall men hardly show their well-proved mettle. They seem astonished to see before them these familiar flags of their old antagonists, not having thought

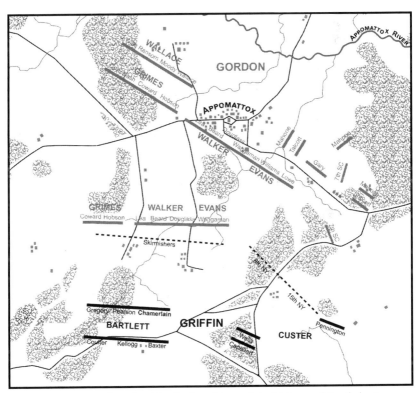

The Last Moments of Battle—The final positions of the Union and Confederate armies near Appomattox Courthouse at the moment of surrender. Note the proximity of Chamberlain's command nearest the center of the Confederate line.

it possible that we could match our cavalry and march around and across their pressing columns.

Their last hope is gone,—to break through our cavalry before our infantry can get up. Neither to Danville nor to Lynchburg can they cut their way; and close upon their rear, five miles away, are pressing the Second and Sixth Corps of the Army of the Potomac. It is the end! They are now giving way, but keep good front, by force of old habit. Half way up the slope they make a stand, with what perhaps they think a good omen,— behind a stone wall. I try a little artillery on them, which directs their thoughts towards the crest behind them, and stiffen my lines for a rush, anxious for that crest myself. My intensity may have seemed like excitement. For Griffin comes up, quizzing me in his queer way of hitting off our weak points when we get a little too serious; accusing me of mistaking a blooming peach tree for a rebel flag, where I was dropping a few shells into a rallying crowd. I apologize—I was a little near-sighted, and hadn't been experienced in longrange fighting. But as for peaches, I was going to get some if the pits didn't sit too hard on our stomachs.

But now comes up Ord with a positive order: "Don't expose your lines on that crest. The enemy have massed their guns to give it a raking fire the moment you set foot there." I thought I saw a qualifying look as he turned away. But left alone, youth struggled with prudence. My troops were in a bad position down here. I did not like to be "the under dog." It was much better to be on top and at least know what there was beyond. So I thought of Grant and his permission to "push things" when we got them going; and of Sheridan and his last words as he rode away with his cavalry, smiting his hands together—"Now smash 'em, I tell you; smash em!" So we took this for orders, and on the crest we stood. One booming cannon-shot passed close along our front, and in the next moment all was still.

We had done it,—had "exposed ourselves to the view of the enemy." But it was an exposure that worked two ways. For there burst upon our vision a mighty scene, fit cadence of the story of tumultuous years. Encompassed by the cordon of steel that crowned the heights about the courthouse, on the slopes of the valley formed by the sources of the Appomattox, lay the remnants of that far-famed army, counterpart and companion of our own in momentous history,—the Army of Northern Virginia—Lee's army!

It was hilly, broken ground, in effect a vast amphitheatre, stretching a mile perhaps from crest to crest. On the several confronting slopes before us dusky masses of infantry suddenly resting in place; blocks of artillery, standing fast in column or mechanically swung into park; clouds of cavalry, small and great, slowly moving, in simple restlessness;—all without apparent attempt at offence or defence, or even military order.

In the hollow is the Appomattox,—which we had made the dead-line for our baffled foe, for its whole length, a hundred miles; here but a rivulet that might almost be stepped over dry-shod, and at the road crossing not thought worth while to bridge. Around its edges, now trodden to mire, swarms an indescribable crowd: worn-out soldier struggling to the front; demoralized citizen and denizen, white, black, and all shades between,—following Lee's army, or flying before these suddenly confronted, terrible Yankees pictured to them as demon-shaped and bent; animals too, of all forms and grades; vehicles of every description and non-description,—public and domestic, four-wheeled, or two, or one,—heading and moving in every direction, a swarming mass of chaotic confusion.

All this within sight of every eye on our bristling crest. Had one the heart to strike at beings so helpless, the Appomattox would quickly become a surpassing Red Sea horror. But the very spectacle brings every foot to an instinctive halt. We seem the possession of a dream. We are lost in a vision of human tragedy. But our lighttwelve Napoleon guns come rattling up behind us to go into battery; we catch the glitter of the cavalry blades and brasses beneath the oak groves away to our right, and the ominous closing in on the fated foe.

So with a fervor of devout joy,—as when, perhaps, the old crusaders first caught sight of the holy city of their quest,—with an up-going of the heart that was half paen, half prayer, we dash forward to the consummation. A solitary field-piece in the edge of the town gives an angry but expiring defiance. We press down a little slope, through a little swamp, over a bright swift stream. Our advance is already in the town,—only the narrow street between the opposing lines, and hardly that. There is wild work, that looks like fighting; but not much killing, nor even hurting. The disheartened enemy take it easy; our men take them easier. It is a wild, mild fusing,—earnest, but not deadly earnest.

A young orderly of mine, unable to contain himself, begs permission to go forward, and dashes in, sword-flourishing as if he were a terrible fellow,—his demonstrations seemingly more amusing than resisted; for he soon comes back, hugging four sabres to his breast, speechless at his achievement.

We were advancing,—tactically fighting,—and I was somewhat mazed as to how much more of the strenuous should be required or expected. But I could not give over to this weak mood.

My right was "in the air," advanced, unsupported, towards the enemy's general line, exposed to flank attack by troops I could see in the distance across the stream. I held myself on that extreme flank, where I could see the cavalry which we had relieved, now forming in column of squadrons ready for a dash to the front, and I was anxiously hoping it would save us from the flank attack. Watching intently, my eye was caught by the figure of a horseman riding out between those lines, soon joined by another, and taking a direction across the cavalry front towards our position. They were nearly a mile away, and I curiously watched them till lost from sight in the nearer broken ground and copses between. Suddenly rose to sight another form, close in our own front,—a soldierly young figure, handsomely dressed and mounted,—a Confederate staff-officer undoubtedly, to whom some of my advanced line seemed to be pointing my position. Now I see the white flag earnestly borne, and its possible purport sweeps before my inner vision like a wraith of morning mist. He comes steadily on,—the mysterious form in gray, my mood so whimsically sensitive that I could even smile at the material of the flag,—wondering where in either army was found a towel, and one so white. But it bore a mighty message,—that simple emblem of homely service, wafted hitherward above the dark and crimsoned streams that never can wash themselves away.

The messenger draws near, dismounts; with graceful salutation and hardly suppressed emotion delivers his message: "Sir, I am from General Gordon. General Lee desires a cessation of hostilities until he can hear from General Grant as to the proposed surrender."

What word is this! so long so dearly fought for, so feverishly dreamed, but ever snatched away, held hidden and aloof; now smiting the senses with a dizzy flash! "Surrender"? We had no rumor of this from the messages that had been passing between Grant and Lee, for now these two days, behind us. "Surrender"? It takes a moment to gather one's speech. "Sir," I answer, "that matter exceeds my authority. I will send to my superior. General Lee is right. He can do no more." All this with a forced calmness, covering a tumult of heart and brain. I bid him wait a while, and the message goes up to my corps commander, General Griffin, leaving me mazed at the boding change.

Now from the right come foaming up in cavalry fashion the two forms I had watched from away beyond. A white flag again, held strong aloft, making straight for the little group beneath our battle-flag, high borne also,—the red Maltese cross on a field of white, that had thrilled hearts long ago. I see now that it is one of our cavalry staff in lead,—indeed I recognize him, Colonel Whitaker of Custer's staff; and, hardly keeping pace with him, a Confederate staff-officer.

Without dismounting, without salutation, the cavalryman shouts: "This is unconditional surrender! This is the end!" Then he hastily introduces his companion, and adds: "I am just from Gordon and Longstreet. Gordon says 'For God's sake, stop this infantry, or hell will be to pay!' I'll go to Sheridan," he adds, and dashes away with the white flag, leaving Longstreet's aide with me.*

I was doubtful of my duty. The flag of truce was in, but I had no right to act upon it without orders. There was still some firing from various quarters, lulling a little where the white flag passed near. But I did not press things quite so hard. Just then a last cannon-shot from the edge of the town plunges through the breast of a gallant and dear young officer in my front line,— Lieutenant Clark, of the 185th New York,—the last man killed in the Army of the Potomac, if not the last in the Appomattox lines. Not a strange thing for war,—this swift stroke of the mortal; but coming after the truce was in, it seemed a cruel fate for one so deserving to share his country's joy, and a sad peace-offering for us all.

Shortly comes the order, in due form, to cease firing and to halt. There was not much firing to cease from; but "halt," then and there? It is beyond human power to stop the men, whose one word and thought and action through crimsoned years had been but forward. They had seen the flag of truce, and could divine its outcome. But the habit was too strong; they cared not for points of direction, but it was forward still,—forward to the end; forward to the new beginning; forward to the Nation's second birth! But it struck them also in a quite human way. The more the captains cry "Halt! the rebels want to surrender," the more the men want to be there and see it. Still to the front, where the real fun is! And the forward takes an upward turn. For when we do succeed in stopping their advance, we cannot keep their arms and legs from flying.

To the top of fences, and haystacks, and chimneys they clamber, to toss their old caps higher in the air, and leave the earth as far below them as they can. Dear old General Gregory gallops up to inquire the meaning of this strange departure from accustomed discipline. "Only that Lee wants time to surrender," I answer with stage solemnity. "Glory to God!" roars the grave and brave old General, dashing upon me with impetuosity that nearly unhorsed us both, to grasp and wring my hand, which had not yet

---

* Chamberlain: "I think the first Confederate officer who came was Captain P. M. Jones, now U.S. District Judge in Alabama; the other, Captain Brown of Georgia."

had time to lower the sword. "Yes, and on earth peace, good will towards men," I answered, bringing the thanksgiving from heavenward, manward.

"Your legs have done it, my men," shouts the gallant, gray-haired Ord, galloping up cap in hand, generously forgiving our disobedience of orders, and rash "exposure" on the dubious crest. True enough, their legs had done it,—had "matched the cavalry" as Grant admitted, had cut around Lee's best doings, and commanded the grand halt. But other things too had "done it"; the blood was still fresh upon the Quaker Road, the White Oak Ridge, Five Forks, Farmville, High Bridge, and Sailor's Creek; and we take somewhat gravely this compliment of our new commander, of the Army of the James. At last, after "pardoning something to the spirit of liberty," we get things "quiet along the lines."

A truce is agreed upon until one o'clock,—it is now ten. A conference is to be held,—or rather colloquy, for no one here is authorized to say anything about the terms of surrender. Six or eight officers from each side meet between the lines, near the courthouse, waiting Lee's answer to Grant's summons to surrender. There is lively chat here on this unaccustomed opportunity for exchange of notes and queries.

The first greetings are not all so dramatic as might be thought, for so grave an occasion. "Well, Billy, old boy, how goes it?" asks one loyal West Pointer of a classmate he had been fighting for four years. "Bad, bad, Charlie, bad I tell you; but have you got any whisky?" was the response,—not poetic, not idealistic, but historic; founded on fact as to the strength of the demand, but without evidence of the questionable maxim that the demand creates the supply. More of the economic truth was manifest that scarcity enhances value.

Everybody seems acquiescent, and for the moment cheerful,—except Sheridan. He does not like the cessation of hostilities, and does not conceal his opinion. His natural disposition was not sweetened by the circumstance that he was fired on by some of the Confederates as he was coming up to the meeting under the truce. He is for unconditional surrender, and thinks we should have banged right on and settled all questions without asking them. He strongly intimates that some of the free-thinking rebel cavalry might take advantage of the truce to get away from us. But the Confederate officers, one and all, Gordon, Wilcox, Heth, "Rooney" Lee, and all the rest assure him of their good faith, and that the game is up for them.

But suddenly a sharp firing cuts the air about our ears,—musketry and artillery,—out beyond us on the Lynchburg pike, where it seems Sheridan had sent Gregg's command to stop any free-riding pranks that might be played. Gordon springs up from his pile of rails with an air of astonishment and vexation, declaring that for his part he had sent out in good faith orders to hold things as they are. And he glances more than inquiringly at Sheridan. "Oh, never mind," says Sheridan, "I know about it. Let 'em fight!" with two simple words added, which literally taken are supposed to express a condemnatory judgment, but in Sheridan's rhetoric convey his appreciation of highly satisfactory qualities of his men,—especially just now.

One o'clock comes; no answer from Lee. Nothing for us but to shake hands and take arms to resume hostilities. As I turned to go, General Griffin said to me in a low voice, "Prepare to make, or receive, an attack in ten minutes!" It was a sudden change of tone in our relations, and brought a queer sensation. Where my troops had halted, the opposing lines were in close proximity. The men had stacked arms and were resting in place. It did not seem like war we were to recommence, but wilful murder. But the order was only to "prepare," and that we did. Our troops were in good position,—my advanced line across the road; and we stood fast intensely waiting. I had mounted and sat looking at the scene before me, thinking of all that was impending and depending; when I felt coming in upon me a strange sense of some presence invisible but powerful like those unearthly visitants told of in ancient story, charged with supernal message.

Disquieted, I turned about; and there behind me, riding in between my two lines, appeared a commanding form, superbly mounted, richly accoutred; of imposing bearing, noble countenance, with expression of deep sadness overmastered by deeper strength. It is no other than Robert E. Lee! And seen by me for the first time within my own lines. I sat immovable, with a certain awe and admiration. He was coming, with a single staff-officer [Col. Marshall, chief of staff] for the great appointed meeting which was to determine momentous issues.

Not long after, by another inleading road, appeared another form— plain, unassuming, simple, and familiar to our eyes; but to the thought as much inspiring awe as Lee in his splendor and his sadness. It is Grant! He, too, comes with a single aide,—a staff-officer of Sheridan's [Col. Newhall]. Slouched hat without cord; common soldier's blouse, un-buttoned, on which, however, the four stars; high boots, mud-splashed to the top, trousers tucked inside; no sword, but the sword-hand deep in the pocket; sitting his saddle with the ease of a born master; taking no notice of anything, all his faculties gathered into intense thought and mighty calm. He seemed greater than I had ever seen him,—a look as of another world about him. No wonder I forgot altogether to salute him. Anything like that would have been too little.

He rode on to meet Lee at the courthouse. What momentous issues had these two souls to declare! Neither of them, in truth, free, nor held in individual bounds alone; no longer testing each other's powers and resources; no longer weighing the chances of daring or desperate conflict. Instruments of God's hands, they were now to record His decree!

But the final word is not long coming now. Staff officers are flying, crying "Lee surrenders!" Ah, there was some kind of strength left among those worn and famished men belting the hills around the springs of the Appomattox, who rent the air with shouting and uproar, as if earth and sea had joined the song. Our men did what they thought their share, and then went to sleep, as they had need to do; but in the opposite camp they acted as if they had got hold of something too good to keep, and gave it to the stars.

Besides, they had a supper that night,—which was something of a novelty. For we had divided rations with our old antagonists now that they were by our side as suffering brothers. In truth, Longstreet had come over to our camp that evening, with an unwonted moisture on his martial cheek and compressed words on his lips: "Gentlemen, I must speak plainly; we are starving over there. For God's sake, can you send us something?" We were men; and we acted like men, knowing we should suffer for it ourselves. We were too short-rationed also, and had been for days, and must be for days to come. But we forgot Andersonville and Belle Isle that night, and sent over to that starving camp share and share alike for all there with ourselves; nor thinking the merits of the case diminished by the circumstance that part of these provisions was what Sheridan had captured from their trains the night before.

At last we sleep—those who can. And so ended that 9th of April, 1865,—Palm Sunday—in that obscure little Virginia village now blazoned for immortal fame. Graver destinies were determined on that humble field than on many of classic and poetic fame. And though the issue brought bitterness to some, yet the heart of humanity the world over thrilled at the tidings. To us, I know, who there fell asleep that night, amidst memories of things that never can be told, it came like that Palm Sunday of old, when the rejoicing multitude met the meekly riding King, and cried "Peace in Heaven; glory in the highest!"

Late that night I was summoned to headquarters, where General Griffin informed me that I was to command the parade on the occasion of the formal surrender of the arms and colors of Lee's army. He said the Confederates had begged hard to be allowed to stack their arms on the ground where they were, and let us go and pick them up after they had gone; but that Grant did not think this quite respectful enough to anybody, including the United States of America; and while he would have all private property respected, and would permit officers to retain their side arms, he insisted that the surrendering army as such should march out in due order, and lay down all tokens of Confederate authority and organized hostility to the United States, in immediate presence of some representative portion of the Union army. Griffin added in a significant tone that Grant wished the ceremony to be as simple as possible, and that nothing should be done to humiliate the manhood of the Southern soldiers.

We felt this honor, but fain would share it. We missed our Second and Sixth Corps. They were only three miles away, and just moving back to Burkeville. We could not but feel something more than a wish that they should be brought up to be participants in a consummation to which they perhaps more than any had contributed. But whatever of honor or privilege came to us of the Fifth Corps was accepted not as for any pre-eminent work or worth of ours, but in the name of the whole noble Army of the Potomac; with loving remembrance of every man, whether on horse or foot or cannon-caisson, whether with shoulder-strap of office or of knapsack,—of every man, whether his heart bent high with the joy of this hour, or was long since stilled in the shallow trenches that furrow the red earth from the Antietam to the Appomattox!

On the morning of the 11th our division had been moved over to relieve Turner's of the Twenty-Fourth Corps, Army of the James, near the courthouse, where they had been receiving some of the surrendered arms, especially of the artillery on their front, while Mackenzie's cavalry had received the surrendered sabres of W.H.F. Lee's command.

At noon of the 11th these troops of the Army of the James took up the march to Lynchburg, to make sure of that yet doubtful point of advantage. Lee and Grant had both gone,—Lee for Richmond to see his dying wife, Grant for Washington, only that once more to see again Lincoln living. The business transactions had been settled; the parole papers made out; all was ready for the last turn,—the dissolving-view of the Army of Northern Virginia.

It was now the morning of the 12th of April. I had been ordered to have my lines formed for the ceremony at sunrise. It was a chill gray morning, depressing to the senses. But our hearts made warmth. Great memories uprose; great thoughts went forward. We formed along the principal street, from the bluff bank of the stream to near the courthouse on the left,—to face the last line of battle, and receive the last remnant of the arms and colors of that great army ours had been created to confront for all that death

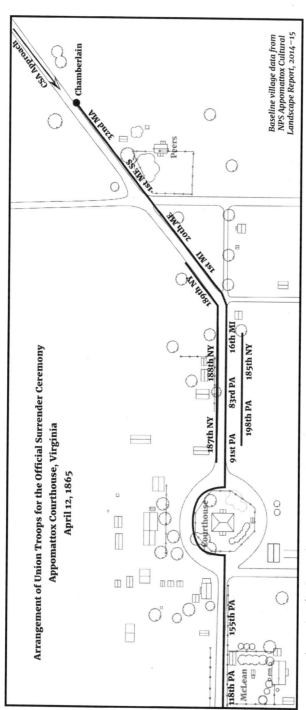

Arrangement of Union Troops for the Official Surrender Ceremony
Appomattox Courthouse, Virginia
April 12, 1865

CSA Approach

Chamberlain

32nd ME

1st ME SS

Peers

20th ME

1st MI

189th NY

188th NY

16th MI

187th NY

83rd PA

185th NY

91st PA

198th PA

Courthouse

155th PA

118th PA

McLean

Baseline village data from
NPS Appomattox Cultural
Landscape Report, 2014–15

Accepting the Surrender—Locations of the 5th Army Corps units that received the surrender of the Confederate infantry.

can do for life. We were remnants also,—Massachusetts, Maine, Michigan, Maryland, Pennsylvania, New York,—veterans, and replaced veterans; cut to pieces, cut down, consolidated, divisions into brigades, regiments into one gathered by State origin, back to their birthplace; this little line—quintessence or metempsychosis of Porter's old corps of Gaines's Mill and Malvern Hill; men of near blood born, made nearer by blood shed. Those facing us—now thank God,—the same.

Our earnest eyes scan the busy groups on the opposite slopes, breaking camp for the last time,—taking down their little shelter-tents and folding them carefully, as precious things, then slowly forming ranks as for unwelcome duty. And now they move. The dusky swarms forge forward into gray columns of march. On they come, with the old swinging route step, and swaying battle-flags. In the van, the proud Confederate ensign,—the great field of white and for canton the star-strewn cross of blue on a field of red, this latter escutcheon also the regimental battle-flags following on crowded so thick, by thinning out of men, that the whole column seemed crowned with red. At the right of our line our little group mounted beneath our flags, the red Maltese cross on a field of white, erewhile so bravely borne through many a field more crimson than itself, its mystic meaning now ruling all.

This was the last scene of such momentous history that I was impelled to render some token of recognition; some honor also to manhood so high.

Instructions had been given; and when the head of each division column comes opposite our group, our bugle sounds the signal and instantly our whole line from right to left, regiment by regiment in succession, gives the soldier's salutation,—from the "order arms" to the old "carry" the marching salute. Gordon at the head of the column, riding with heavy spirit and downcast face, catches the sound of shifting arms, looks up, and, taking the meaning, wheels superbly, making with himself and his horse one uplifted figure, with profound salutation as he drops the point of his sword to the boot toe; then facing to his own command, gives word for his successive brigades to pass us with the same position of the manual,—honor answering honor. On our part not a sound of trumpet more, nor roll of drum; not a cheer, nor word nor whisper of vain-glorying, nor motion of man standing again at the order; but an awed stillness rather and breath-holding, as if it were the passing of the dead!

As each successive division masks our own, it halts the men face inward towards us across the road, twelve feet away; then carefully "dress" their line, each captain taking pains for the good appearance of his company, worn and torn and half starved as they were. The field and staff take their positions in the intervals of regiments; generals in rear of their commands. They fix bayonets, stack arms; then, hesitatingly, remove cartridge-boxes and lay them down. Lastly,— reluctantly, with agony of expression,—they tenderly fold their flags, battle-worn and torn, blood-stained, heart-holding colors, and lay them down; some frenziedly rushing from the ranks, kneeling over them, clinging to them, pressing them to their lips with burning tears. And only the Flag of the Union greets the sky!

What visions thronged as we looked into each others' eyes! Here pass the men of Antietam, the Bloody Lane, the Sunken Road, the Cornfield, the Burnside-Bridge; the men whom Stonewall Jackson on the second night at Fredericksburg begged Lee to let him take and crush the two corps of the Army of the Potomac huddled in the streets in darkness and confusion; the men who swept away the Eleventh Corps at Chancellorsville; who left six thousand of their companions around the bases of Culp's and Cemetery Hills at Gettysburg; these survivors of the terrible Wilderness, the Bloody-Angle at Spotsylvania, the slaughter pen of Cold Harbor, the whirlpool of Bethesda Church!

Here comes Cobb's Georgia Legion, which held the stonewall on Marye's Heights at Fredericksburg, close before which we piled our dead for breastworks so that the living might stay and live.

Here too come Gordon's Georgians and Hoke's North Carolinians, who stood before the terrific mine explosion at Petersburg, and advancing retook the smoking crater and the dismal heaps of dead—ours more than theirs—huddled in the ghastly chasm.

Here are the men of McGowan, Hunton, and Scales, who broke the Fifth Corps lines on the White Oak Road, and were so desperately driven back on that forlorn night of March 31st by my thrice-decimated brigade.

Now comes Anderson's Fourth Corps,—only Bushrod Johnson's division left, and this the remnant of those we fought so fiercely on the Quaker Road, two weeks ago, with Wise's Legion, too fierce for its own good.

Here passes the proud remnant of Ransom's North Carolinians we swept through Five Forks ten days ago,—and all the little that was left of this division in the sharp passages at Sailor's Creek five days thereafter. Now makes its last front A. P. Hill's old corps,—[Gen. Henry] Heth now at the head, since Hill had gone too far forward ever to return: the men who poured destruction into our division at Shepardstown Ford, Antietam, in '62, when Hill reported the Potomac running blue with our bodies; the men who opened the desperate first day's fight at Gettysburg, where withstanding them so stubbornly our [Gen. John C.] Robinson's brigades lost 1185 men, and the Iron Brigade alone 1153,—these men of Heth's division here too losing 2850 men, companions of these now looking into our faces so differently.

What is this but the remnant of Mahone's division, last seen by us at the North Anna? Its thinned ranks of worn, bright-eyed men recalling scenes of costly valor and ever-remembered history.

Now the sad great pageant,—Longstreet and his men! What shall we give them for greeting that has not already been spoken in volleys of thunder and written in lines of fire on all the river-banks of Virginia? Shall we go back to Gaines's Mill and Malvern Hill? Or to the Antietam of Maryland, or Gettysburg of Pennsylvania?—deepest graven of all. For here is what remains of Kershaw's division, which left 40 per cent. of its men at Antietam, and at Gettysburg with Barksdale's and Semmes's brigades tore through the Peach Orchard, rolling up the right of our gallant Third Corps, sweeping over the proud batteries of Massachusetts,—Bigelow and Philips,—where under the smoke we saw the earth brown and blue with prostrate bodies of horses and men, and the tongues of overturned cannon and caissons pointing grim and stark in the air.

Then in the Wilderness and at Spotsylvania Kershaw again, in deeds of awful glory, and thereafter, for all their losses, holding their name and fame, until fate met them at Sailor's Creek, where all but these, with Kershaw himself, and Ewell, and so many more, gave up their arms and hopes,—all, indeed, but manhood's honor.

With what strange emotion I looked into these faces before which in the mad assault on Rives's Salient, June 18, '64, I was left for dead under their eyes! It is by miracles we have lived to see this day,—any of us standing here.

Now comes the sinewy remnant of fierce Hood's division, which at Gettysburg we saw pouring through the Devil's Den, and the Plum Run gorge; turning again by the left our stubborn Third Corps, then swarming up the rocky bastions of Round Top, to be met there by equal valor, which changed Lee's whole plan of battle, and perhaps the story of Gettysburg. Ah, is this Pickett's division?—this little group, left of those who on the lurid last day of Gettysburg breasted level cross-fire and thunderbolts of storm, to be strewn back drifting wrecks, where after that awful, futile, pitiful charge we buried them in graves a furlong wide, with names unknown!

Met again in the terrible cyclone-sweep over the breastworks at Five Forks; met now, so thin, so pale, purged of the mortal,—as if knowing pain or joy no more. How could we help falling on our knees,—all of us together,—and praying God to pity and forgive us all!

Thus, all day long, division after division comes and goes,—the surrendered arms being removed by our wagons in the intervals, the cartridge-
boxes emptied in the street when the ammunition was found unserviceable,
our men meanwhile resting in place.

When all is over, in the dusk of evening, the long lines of scattered
cartridges are set on fire; and the lurid flames wreathing the blackness of
earthly shadows give an unearthly border to our parting.

Then, stripped of every token of enmity or instrument of power to
hurt, they march off to give their word of honor never to lift arms against
the old flag again till its holders release them from their promise. Then,
their ranks broken,—the bonds that bound them fused away by forces
stronger than fire,—they are free at last to go where they will; to find their
homes, now most likely stricken, despoiled by war.

Twenty-seven thousand men paroled; seventeen thousand stand of
arms laid down or gathered up; a hundred battle-flags. But regiments and
brigades—or what is left of them—have scarce a score of arms to surrender;
having thrown them away by road and riverside in weariness of flight or
hopelessness of heart, disdaining to carry them longer but to disaster. And
many a bare staff was there laid down, from which the ensign had been
torn in the passion and struggle of emotions, and divided piece by piece,—a
blurred or shrunken star, a rag of smoke-stained blue from the war-worn
cross, a shred of deepened dye from the rent field of red,—to be treasured
for precious keepsakes of manhood's test and heirlooms for their children.

Nor blame them too much for this; nor us for not blaming them
more. Although, as we believed, fatally wrong in striking at the old flag,
misreading its deeper meaning and the innermost law of the people's life,
blind to the signs of the times in the march of man, they fought as they
were taught, true to such ideals as they saw, and put into their cause their
best. For us they were fellow-soldiers as well, suffering the fate of arms.
We could not look into those brave, bronzed faces, and those battered flags
we had met on so many fields where glorious manhood lent a glory to the
earth that bore it, and think of personal hate and mean revenge. Whoever
had misled these men, we had not. We had led them back, home. Whoever
had made that quarrel, we had not. It was a remnant of the inherited curse
for sin. We had purged it away, with blood-offerings. We were all of us
together factors of that high will which, working often through illusions
of the human, and following ideals that lead through storms, evolves the
enfranchisement of man.

Forgive us, therefore, if from stern, steadfast faces eyes dimmed with
tears gazed at each other across that pile of storied relics so dearly there laid

down, and brothers' hands were fain to reach across that rushing tide of memories which divided us yet made us forever one.

It was our glory only that the victory we had won was for country; for the well-being of others, of these men before us as well as for ourselves and ours. Our joy was a deep, far, unspoken satisfaction,—the approval, as it were, of some voiceless and veiled divinity like the appointed "Angel of the Nation" of which the old scriptures tell—leading and looking far, yet mindful of sorrows; standing above all human strife and fierce passages of trial; not marking faults nor seeking blame; transmuting into factors of the final good corrected errors and forgiven sins; assuring of immortal inheritance all pure purpose and noble endeavor, humblest service and costliest sacrifice, unconscious and even mistaken martyrdoms offered and suffered for the sake of man.